Advanced
PROJECT
MANAGEMENT

*A complete guide to the key processes,
models and techniques*

ALAN D ORR

**KOGAN
PAGE**

London and Philadelphia

First published in Great Britain and the United States in 2004 by Kogan Page Limited
Paperback edition 2007
Reprinted 2007

120 Pentonville Road
London N1 9JN
United Kingdom
www.kogan-page.co.uk

525 South 4th Street, #241
Philadelphia PA 19147
USA

© Alan D Orr, 2004

ISBN-10   0 7494 4983 7
ISBN-13   978 0 7494 4983 4

British Library Cataloguing-in-Publication Data

A CIP record for this book is available from the British Library.

Library of Congress Cataloging-in-Publication Data

Orr, Alan.
    Advanced project management : a complete guide to the processes, models and techniques/Alan Orr.
        p. cm.
    Includes index.
    ISBN-13: 978-0-7494-4983-4
    ISBN-10: 0-7494-4983-7
    1. Project management. I. Title.
    HD69.P75O77 2007
    658.4'04—dc22

                                        2007005278

Typeset by JS Typesetting Ltd, Porthcawl, Mid Glamorgan
Printed and bound in Great Britain by Creative Print and Design (Wales), Ebbw Vale

Contents

Introduction

In today's highly competitive market, project management has become one of the most valued skills in all types of organizations. To thrive, it is essential that organizations deliver their projects on time. No matter what method organizations choose, they rely heavily on the expertise of skilled project managers. This is especially the case when organizations undertake a major project where they need project managers with advanced skills.

This book has been written to help project managers to revise and advance their skills. It is for project managers who are or will be managing projects involving multiple disciplines and substantial resource. You will be taken through all of the key skills that you will need to ensure that you deliver your project successfully. The book covers all of the key areas of project management with a particular focus on the perspective that a project manager should have at any moment in time.

Whilst many of the skills learnt by intermediate-level project managers still apply, such as basic Gantt chart manipulation, there are new skills to learn. This book explains those skills, setting out processes, methods and tools to enable a smooth and successful project delivery, for example how to handle the much larger volume of requirements and change that occurs in complex projects, and what to do when you can no longer deal with every change personally.

Key topics that will be blended throughout the book include how to handle the many stakeholders who will undoubtedly have an interest in the project. In particular it explains the difference between gathering information for managing the project and gathering information for managing stakeholders. Project managers can gain control not only of their projects but also of their organizations' needs.

Projects follow a natural series of steps that takes them from their inception to their close. These natural steps have been used as the basis for the order of this book. Each chapter takes you closer to the end of the project. At each stage the key concepts and techniques are introduced and often examples are given. The chapters are:

- Chapter 1: Starting an advanced project successfully;
- Chapter 2: Building the macro plan;
- Chapter 3: Building the detailed project plan;
- Chapter 4: Building the project team;
- Chapter 5: How to run the project on a day-to-day basis;
- Chapter 6: Monitoring and controlling the project;
- Chapter 7: Successfully shutting down the project;
- Chapter 8: Emergency actions.

Chapter 1: Starting an advanced project successfully covers the initiation of the project. At this stage in the project's lifetime it can seem impossible that the project will ever start, much less complete. This chapter explains how to overcome the mass of ideas and work that could be undertaken and shows you how to focus on four key themes. These themes are the underlying themes for the majority of project life cycles. They are:

1. Stakeholder management.
2. Build the business case.
3. Start long-lead activities.
4. Define early roles and responsibilities.

Correct management and control of these themes will ensure successful transition through the early project stages. In practice these themes occur throughout the project in some guise and therefore they are returned to several times during the text.

Chapter 2: Building the macro plan explains how to move past the initial stages where there are only ideas and no plans. It describes how to set out a macro plan that explains the detail and the strategy associated with that detail. This chapter covers how to gain the commitment of managers and the buy-in of staff to the plans. Taking forward the initial themes, the chapter shows you how to change them into a work breakdown structure and then how to manage the completion of the work breakdown structure.

Chapter 3: Building the detailed project plan builds on Chapter 2 and explains how to develop a much more detailed analysis of how the project should be managed. Without a well-written plan you will find it difficult to manage an advanced project. This chapter sets out how to go about the production in a sensible manner. It points out pitfalls and sets out techniques that will save you time and effort. Specifically it sets out how to gather requirements, the building of the associated schedule and finally the production of the project plan.

Chapter 4: Building the project team covers perhaps one of the most important aspects that you can undertake in any project. Initially the text leads you through the way of identifying your team. However, this is quickly developed into methods of motivating the team. It explains the key aspects of successfully dealing with team issues and concludes with how to gain the respect of the project team.

Chapter 5: How to run the project on a day-to-day basis explains the basic fundamentals of what to do day to day. It covers the different ways that a project can be set up and run. In particular, it sets out how to tackle an implementation strategy and then how to execute that strategy. This chapter additionally covers how to ensure that quality remains on the agenda during the execution of the project, an aspect that you should be keen to discover.

Chapter 6: Monitoring and controlling the project covers an area that can prove to be difficult when it is an advanced project you are running. To be successful you need to gather together sufficient information to enable you to understand what is going on but not so much that you stifle those trying to do the work. This chapter explains how to achieve this without ruining all of the hard work undertaken so far.

Chapter 7: Successfully shutting down the project explains an aspect that can be surprisingly difficult. Often those who commissioned the project can find it difficult to allow the project team to move on to other work. They feel that when you and the team move on to other work they will be unable to resolve the numerous tidying-up activities. This chapter shows you how to achieve closure effectively.

Chapter 8: Emergency actions concludes by covering actions that are often necessary in advanced projects. These allow you to recover the project timescales and delivery when things go wrong. This chapter shows you how to run these actions and how to use them successfully.

1

Starting an advanced project successfully

Surprisingly, once an organization has decided to undertake an advanced project, building the initial momentum can be difficult. The number of people involved in the project will grow quickly and as a result it becomes increasingly difficult to make progress. Often the early stages are characterized by significant time wasting. Since time is one of the most valuable commodities, this is something that should be avoided if at all possible. Fortunately a project manager can take effective action. If handled well, the initiation stage will be short and successful.

The accepted way for an organization to ensure a successful project is to adopt a tried-and-tested project life cycle. The life cycle sets out a range of activities that need to be undertaken. It specifies the order in which tasks need to happen and the content of each task. Life cycles also take into account that advanced projects are actually many smaller projects running in parallel. These smaller projects are bound together by the overall project and as a result they all share the same final goal. For example, at the highest level the project might be the building and fit-out of a corporate headquarters. Within this larger project there are many small projects that collectively deliver the necessary parts of the overall project jigsaw. Together the smaller projects result in the achievement of the larger project's goal – a completed headquarters.

Understanding that there are a number of small projects all operating in parallel helps to unlock one of the key problems that needs to be overcome to ensure the success of an advanced project. Each of the small projects operates to its own life cycle and in response the people on these projects all operate in different ways. Those responsible for near-term deliveries (short project timescales and therefore short life cycle) will be agitated about lack of progress. Those with deliveries that are further away (longer project life cycle) will be more relaxed about lack of progress. As a result conflicts can often occur. There will be those, even in the initiation phase, who 'just want to get on with it'. They will be very frustrated at slow methodical planning. It is essential to remember this when dealing with the various project teams. Those attending the various initiation phase meetings are likely to be at different places in their project life cycles. They need to be dealt with appropriately.

The other major difficulty with life cycles within advanced projects is the reliance by senior managers on them. Unfortunately senior managers often come to believe that project life cycles alone deal with the complexities of an advanced project. They often believe that the project life cycle will ensure the success of any project. This is not true. It is the skill of the project manager that will ensure project success, not the project life cycle. The main benefit for any given life cycle is its provision of well-thought-out guidance material. This material helps to ensure that the steps needed to ensure success in the process are not forgotten. Your role is the successful interpretation of the project life cycle tasks. Ultimately it is your interpretation of the project life cycle material that will ensure the success of the project.

You need to understand the true purpose of the life cycle tasks to be completed. This means understanding the underlying themes that must be nurtured to gain the success that the organization is desperately seeking. You should not simply follow the life cycle blindly. Completing the tasks that are detailed in the quality manual will not ensure success. Instead you should consider four themes that almost always are the underlying requirements of the initiation phase. These are the themes that you need to work on first. This means ignoring the letter of the life cycle and operating it within the context of the following four themes:

1. Stakeholder management.
2. Build the business case.
3. Start long-lead activities.
4. Define early roles and responsibilities.

Each of these themes has the potential to take up a significant amount of your time and therefore you need to think carefully about how you will manage them. This is especially true when you are in charge of an advanced project, where the scope and scale of work are usually far greater than for a standard project. In practice you will find it difficult to support all of these themes fully. This obviously presents difficulties for you since the themes will run continuously and in parallel throughout the initiation phase. Ideally you could use extra resource to enable you to cope with the additional work load. However, even if extra help is provided you still need to look after these four themes personally. Personal involvement from you is important since it is these themes that will ensure the project is a success! Despite the difficulty it is possible to cope with these themes by careful time management and by using some of the suggestions in the following discussion on each of the themes.

THEME 1: STAKEHOLDER MANAGEMENT

This theme covers a topic that is often undertaken poorly by project managers. Although many organizations promote the management of stakeholders in projects, this rarely translates into active stakeholder management. This is a mistake since this theme is extremely important and is one that occurs continuously during a project. If stakeholder management is undertaken successfully, the project will run more smoothly. Because this theme is significant it is returned to many times throughout this book.

Project managers often do not understand the benefits to be gained from good stakeholder management. They simply see it as the production of a stakeholder management plan: an activity to be completed in response to the life cycle guidance material. This lack of understanding is often shared by the reviewers of the stakeholder management plan. At the milestone review those present simply check that a stakeholder plan exists. Reviewers often do not concern themselves with the content of the plan. They are more concerned with the content of other documents such as the business case or the project schedule. You, however, must look at the deeper purpose of producing a stakeholder management plan. It should mean far more to you than simply a life cycle milestone requirement. A well-written plan should demonstrate your understanding of the relationships that will ultimately drive the success of the project.

Business planning

The most common reason given, by project managers, for not seriously attempting a stakeholder management plan is lack of available time. Project managers believe that other activities should take priority. They therefore choose to pay little attention to this area and they feel justified in this choice since many organizations accept this as the right decision. Organizations demonstrate this by allowing a project to pass a life cycle mandated milestone review without seeking evidence of stakeholder management. Organizations that do this are missing the fundamental reason for the stakeholder management plan.

The purpose of the stakeholder management plan is to ensure that the relationships between the principal people in the project have been discussed and the information flow between them agreed. Ironically, it often these principals who don't value a stakeholder management plan. They are the ones who allow the relaxation of the project milestone. They are also the people who complain that the relationships don't work and that they are not kept properly informed.

You do not need to follow this way of working. Instead you can follow a simple process that should result in successful stakeholder management. You can reap the benefits of a plan without the need for large amounts of your time. You can forestall the problems that will occur if stakeholders aren't managed properly.

Completing a simple form like the one shown in Table 1.1 is the first step in a simplified stakeholder management process. This form defines the various stakeholders and their involvement. It is likely that you will need less information for this form than the information required by a formal life cycle for a stakeholder management plan. This form aims to elicit only the key information that you will need. The content sought by the form should be viewed by you as the minimum required for good stakeholder management. It is helpful if this form is created in an electronic format such as a spreadsheet or a database. This allows data to be sorted easily.

Once completed the information on the form should be sorted, first by the supporter column, then by the influence column and finally by the involvement column. A picture should now form in your mind about the various people involved in the project. You should now be able to identify those people who don't support the project and its aims. In particular you should try to identify those who have a high level of influence or a high level of involvement but who don't support the project. Once these people are identified you must spend time with them building a strong working relationship. It is essential that you use this developing relationship as a method for understanding the reasons for the lack of support. You must then try to deal successfully with those reasons and in the process change a detractor into a supporter. The skills that you need here are discussed in

Table 1.1 Stakeholder assessment form

Name (or Group)	Description	Involvement	Influence	Motivation	Supporter	Comments
A Jones	Project sponsor	High	High	Needs new customer booking system to meet overall business strategy	Yes	
Z Nathan	Software director	High	High	Wants his department to be seen as a success and be able to gain personal glory	Sort of	Supports if he can share or take the glory
N Blem	Resource user	Medium	High	Is using some of the same resources for maintenance of existing system	Sort of	Fine as long as her project comes first – her bonus is based on it
S Farrell	System buyer	Low	Low	Job to ensure contract price is negotiated well	Agnostic	Doesn't care as long as his job isn't made difficult by project
Project B	Providing another system	Low	Medium	Providing another system as part of the overall company strategy	Sort of	Fine as long as it doesn't steal the glory from their system

Chapter 4, which explains the fundamental methods of building a team.

In its raw state it is not appropriate for this stakeholder management form to be seen by anyone other than you. It could be interpreted as being deliberately antagonistic towards people or groups within the project. Suggesting someone doesn't support a project that is likely to be of strategic importance to an organization can be very damaging to morale. Therefore you should resist the temptation to submit this form as a cut-down version of the required stakeholder management plan. If you do not have time to complete a stakeholder management plan it is better to submit simply nothing than submit this form in its raw state. However, translating this form into a stakeholder management plan should be a relatively simple task. You should edit the form, removing phrases such as 'doesn't support the project' or 'is always difficult about providing resources'. You must remember that the stakeholders are part of the project and as such they deserve to be treated with respect. Treating the stakeholders with respect regardless of their views will help to make the project successful.

In concluding this theme, it is worth emphasizing again the importance of stakeholder management. Strong relationships with the principals within a project are essential for a project manager. These relationships will not become strong on their own. Instead they will need to be nurtured and worked on throughout the project. The stakeholder management plan is simply a handy tool that can be used to work out and write down the stakeholders' needs. So at this stage if you choose to do nothing else on stakeholder management you should complete the form given for the main principals. This form should be kept private and you should review it every few days as the project initiation phase progresses.

THEME 2: BUILD THE BUSINESS CASE

Building a business case is one of the key parts during the initiation phase of any advanced project. Badly produced business cases will make organizations very nervous. This is particularly true of advanced projects because of the very large investments that are often involved. If the case is badly written then it is likely that the company will continue to prevaricate about the project. This will result in more time being used than is necessary before the project is fully commissioned. It is therefore extremely important that you ensure that the business case is produced efficiently and to the highest standards.

Normally the business case is the responsibility of the project sponsor and because of this many project managers feel that they should not waste time working on it. They do not believe that it is their responsibility to ensure its success. Instead project managers spend their time working on the other three initiation phase project themes: stakeholder management, long-lead item tasks and early roles and responsibility definitions. You should not do this. In advanced projects you cannot leave the success of the business case to someone else. Regardless of whose responsibility it is to complete the business case it is too important for you to ignore it. You must get actively involved in the production of the business case since it is this document that will normally secure you the needed project resources. Actively supporting the project sponsor in the project's business case production is something that you must do.

Often the project sponsor will welcome any offer of support in the production of the business case. However, whilst this enthusiasm will make it easy for you to become involved, you need to exercise caution. Many projects have floundered because project managers and their teams have, wrongly, taken over the production of the business case. Frequently this is done with good intentions, for example to try to ensure that the business case production remains on target. However, despite project managers' good intentions it can end up leaving the project sponsors feeling sidelined. As a result the project sponsors sometimes withhold their signature when it comes to the final approval. Skilful project managers must ensure that this does not happen.

To ensure that project sponsors feel that they are driving the process, you must approach the business case production in a methodical manner. This can be difficult since people are often very unsure at the start of an advanced project about the detail of what they want to achieve. Project sponsors can explain their desired strategy but normally they cannot explain any of the detail. This is unfortunate since project sponsors are also the people who want to see the detail before they are willing to support the case for committing substantial resources. This is a natural way of acting for most people. In general people find it difficult to commit to a high-level strategy without it being backed by significant amounts of detail. They want to be able to understand on a practical level the tasks and activities. Unfortunately this can prove very frustrating for project managers. They are working on something that is not their responsibility and they are being told that the result is not detailed enough.

To overcome the difficulties and get the business case successfully produced you should follow two simple steps. These steps are normally independent of the life cycle being used: 1) Meet the project sponsor. 2) Set up a project steering group.

Meet the project sponsor

Arranging a meeting with the project sponsor and building a strong rapport with the sponsor is the first step to establishing a successful path to the completion of the business case. By the end of your first meeting you should have established a number of goals. These goals should lead to the completion of the business case. At this stage the goals can be set out simply on a sheet of paper with three or four dates against which measurable outputs have been defined. It is possible that at the end of this first meeting the dates and activities will not be fully agreed. When this happens a follow-up meeting should be arranged before you leave the first meeting. As a minimum it is recommended that the outcome of the first meeting is a draft of the business plan production schedule. A suitable form for capturing the schedule, with some sample text, is shown in Figure 1.1.

At first glance the format of the plan might seem odd, but with minimum work it is simple to understand. The chart shows a

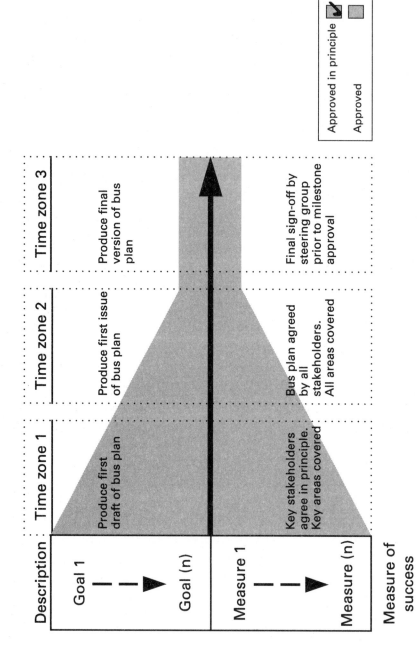

Figure 1.1 Business plan production schedule

funnel lying on its side. This is to indicate the lack of understanding at the beginning of the business plan production. The funnel indicates this improving over time towards clarity at the end of the business plan production. The funnel is included to remind you that you don't have to understand everything at the first meeting.

Along the top of the chart are three time zones (more could be added but three is normally sufficient). These time zones group together the uncertainty about the project requirements. Uncertainty in these requirements means that the project cannot provide details about the implementation. This means that any business case produced at this stage will be fuzzy in its justification for the project. Therefore it is acceptable for the goals and associated measures for the tasks in zone 1 to show reasonable uncertainty in the project requirements. For example, this could mean a large number of requirements being missed from the initial project requirements list. As the work progresses, however, the clarity should improve. By the time the business plan production reaches zone 3 the clarity should have improved dramatically. The goals and associated measures for zone 3 should be clear and unambiguous. When zone 3 has been exited there should exist a clear understanding of what the project must ultimately deliver.

Once you have agreed with the project sponsor the production plan for the business case you next need to help the sponsor develop the material to allow the business case to be written. In some cases this will mean only the production of a very simple paper, perhaps 600 to 1,000 words in length. However, often it means a significant amount of work and the development of a macro plan. The development of the macro plan is a major undertaking and therefore it is dealt with separately in Chapter 2.

Set up a project steering group

At this stage you and the project sponsor should have a business case production plan that you both believe in. This will include sufficient detail to ensure that you are confident of achieving the production of the business case in the given time. It will allow you to argue your case with others to enable you to secure the resources that you need to proceed. However, it is likely that you will now need significant support from others in the organization to enable you to produce the business case. Generally this is achieved by enlisting the help of a project steering group.

Often at this stage a project steering group will not have been formed. If this is the case then you should form the group. In practice it is helpful if you start the formation of this group in parallel to the production of the business case. To form the group you need to gather together a group of senior managers within the organization. These managers need to have significant authority and need to be able to authorize the release of funds or resources to support your project. It is likely that you will already have involved a number of senior people in the project. Normally these people are self-selecting and can be easily coerced into joining the project steering group.

The plan for the business case's production should point you to a date for the presentation of the finalized business case for approval. However, you should not wait until this date before starting to work with the steering group and its members. Instead you need to spend time with the various members of the group explaining in detail the business case. As you explain the detail you should seek their opinion and you should then use that to influence the content of the business case and its production. Prior to the first steering group meeting you and the project sponsor should agree who the chair will be. This is normally the most senior manager present or sometimes the project sponsor. You should meet with the proposed chairperson and explain the business plan production schedule in detail and the different opinions that you have heard from the other steering group members.

At the first meeting of the steering group the project sponsor should present the business case production schedule. The sponsor should be clear what he or she is seeking from the steering group. Generally this will be resources, funds, hardware, etc to enable the business case to be produced. Often this requires a short paper seeking approval in principle for the project. It will set out the basic resources required in order to progress to a full business case and associated project plan. If you, and the project sponsor, have properly briefed the steering group then the outcome of the meeting should be a formality. The meeting should result in the approval of the business case production schedule and the initial paper seeking basic resources in support of the full business case and project plan. When approval has been achieved you can normally take this as a good indication that you have gained senior management support for the project.

THEME 3: START LONG-LEAD ACTIVITIES

One theme that is often overlooked during the early stages of advanced projects is the starting of activities that are likely to take significant time to complete. Often those involved in the project get caught up in the whirlwind that accompanies the business case and other project set-up activities. Project managers often feel that they need to get past the initial approval of the steering group before they can start any activities. Project managers assuming this are wrong.

Advanced projects require you, the project manager, to take risks. During the initiation stage of the project this means starting activities before they are approved. This doesn't mean that you should start every activity that the project requires. Instead you should carefully select those activities that need early attention. Once you have identified the tasks you should approach suitable line managers in the work area most likely to undertake the task. You then need to convince those managers to help you by giving you unapproved resources. The managers you approach are likely to fall into one of two categories. Either they will be very keen to help or they will be completely ambivalent to helping out.

Managers who are keen to start work should obviously be encouraged. However, you must be careful to ensure that they have well-defined boundaries. These boundaries must be sufficient to ensure that the managers concerned have a clear understanding of what is and isn't acceptable. This can be achieved through the use of a straightforward agreement. Figure 1.2 shows a template for a simple form that you can use to make this agreement. This form includes the basic information that should be discussed and agreed between the line manager and yourself.

Since this is an informal agreement it can be tempting to ignore it. However, it often proves to be an effective way of ensuring that work goes smoothly. It provides a focus for discussions between you and the line manager who is undertaking the work. It allows both of you a reliable format that ensures that all of the necessary topics have been discussed.

Completing the form can normally be achieved in a single meeting. It can be helpful if the form is completed electronically. This enables it to be quickly published and ensures that traceability is easy to achieve. The sections of the report are equal in terms of their relative importance. This means that you should give equal weight to completing each of the sections. When completing the form you should remember that this is only initial work. You should therefore set the timescales for completion appropriately.

At some stage during the initiation phase you should formally seek approval for this work from the project steering group. Often the first few meetings of the group are too busy to enable work agreements to be considered and therefore it may be the third or fourth meeting before approval is possible. Nevertheless the work agreement must be tabled for formal approval. As an absolute minimum there should be a review of the work agreement upon approval of the business case.

The same process should be followed for managers who are ambivalent to the project and who aren't keen to be involved in work at this early stage. Chapter 4 covers some of the methods that you can adopt to overcome the reluctance of these managers. Ultimately if they won't commit to giving unapproved resources you will have to delay the work and get authority from the steering group.

Work Agreement
Reference number: NN/NN/NN/NN **Date:** DD/MM/YY

Description

Add a brief description of the activities that will be undertaken. This should specify the purpose of the work and the method by which that purpose will be met.
For example: The task is the early prototyping of a speech recognition module built through a software modelling technique. The description should include a description of the speech recognition and why it is being undertaken. The description should also include a description of the modelling technique that will be used.

Resources

Add a list of the resources that will be used to complete the work being undertaken. This list should include people, hardware, software, building materials, etc. Using some of the resources may require approval. This approval should be sought from the resource owner, normally a line manager or software director. Where approval is sought and given it should be noted in this section.

Expected outcome

Add to this section a list of measurable deliverables that this work agreement is expected to achieve. These should be as specific and measurable as possible: Specific Measurable Attainable Realistic Timely. They should relate directly to the description given.

Risks

Add here a list of the risks that will occur undertaking this work. Often project managers only include here the obvious risk that the project might not be approved and the work will become worthless. Whilst this is a risk worth mentioning it is certainly not the only risk. Other technical risks should also be mentioned.
For example: The prototype speech recognition software might never work properly and so the project would need to find a new way of achieving the input of text into a computer.

Approvals

Add here the signatures of the project manager, the line manager (and any resource owner if not the line manager). This should be a formality but can prove useful in helping to reinforce that commitment to complete work has been made.

Figure 1.2 Work agreement

When the business case has been approved you should be able to terminate all of these work agreements. Normally this is a natural occurrence since many of the work agreements will have been superseded by other work orders or work packages. These work orders or work packages will have been developed as part of the macro plan production (see Chapter 2).

THEME 4: DEFINE EARLY ROLES AND RESPONSIBILITIES

Unlike the other initiation phase themes, which all start immediately, this final theme generally starts a short time after the project work has begun. This happens because as work progresses more people will become involved in the project. This results in a need for you to gain control of the work being undertaken. This quickly becomes difficult since in advanced projects many people within the organization will be keen to take a leading role. They will be keen to demonstrate to the organization that they are wholly behind the advanced project and its strategic aims. It is essential that you quickly gain and keep control. This means the definition of the roles and responsibilities of the people working on the project. You should consider two aspects: 1) reactive control; 2) proactive control.

Reactive control

Reactive control is gaining control of responsibilities that others assume without your agreement. To achieve this you should set up a mechanism that publishes who's who within the project. If introduced successfully the mechanism will become an effective way of stopping people taking assumed responsibility. Instead they will realize that they need to go through the proper channels to be recognized by project team members as having a particular responsibility.

Setting up a suitable mechanism is a relatively simple task. First you should gather together a list of the people involved in the project. This list should include key information about the people on it. Table 1.2 shows a sample list that can be easily adjusted for use on any project.

If possible you should create the list using a spreadsheet or database program. This allows it to be sorted alphabetically and allows for the easy insertion of new names and associated information. It also enables you to publish the information quickly using e-mail or Internet technology. At this initial stage in the project you should personally retain control of the content of this list. This enables you to ensure that the people who are on the list only have authority and responsibility that you are willing to give them.

Proactive control

Proactive control is gaining control by deliberately appointing people into certain roles and responsibilities. To achieve this you need to seek out appropriate people and appoint them into certain key roles. The roles that should be filled are those that can and will have a significant impact on the early project work. Identifying these roles is a relatively simple task. They are the roles that will be highly active in the initial day-to-day work of the project. They are likely to include the project sponsor, any major resource provider and any senior management interested in the project.

Once key roles have been identified you should spend some time agreeing a suitable role description. This can be very simple in nature and should state clearly what the role's involvement in the project is. At this stage it isn't necessary to go through the formality of writing down the role description. It is more effective to retain the informality that accompanies a lack of paperwork. This helps to reduce the potential barriers that paperwork can introduce to relationship building. However, it is helpful to add a simple description to the project who's who.

Table 1.2 Project who's who

First name	Last name	Title	Project responsibility	Telephone	Location
John	Harwell-Smith-Jones	Software director	Overall direction of software development and ownership of quality of final product	xxx xxx xxx	xxx Building 3
Susan	Smith	Market analyst	Analysis of the marketplace and subsequent contribution to product definition	yyy yyy yyy	x3 Building 9
Rodger	Harnton	Software developer	Lead developer for speech recognition module	zzz zzz zzz	x4 Building 9
Robin	Saxton	Test leader	Test plan production and implemention	xxx yyy yyy	xxx Building 3
George	Ramble	Software developer	Lead developer for PC connectivity software implementation	xxx yyy zzz	xxx Building 3

2

Building the macro plan

Building the macro plan is one of the most important aspects of an advanced project. Once completed, it will follow the project through to its final completion and will be used in the assessment of success post project completion. The macro plan serves many purposes. It supplies an overview to those working on the project of the activities and the order in which they are required. It is also used to convince senior managers in an organization that the project will be successful. However its first job is to supply the information necessary to complete the business case, thereby freeing up the resources needed for the project.

The macro plan on its own is not sufficient to allow the completion of the full business case. This requires the completion of a second stage of planning, the work breakdown structure (WBS). Once completed, the work breakdown structure and the macro plan together will enable you to construct a solid business case. They will also set out the activities and schedule that the project needs to undertake. Not surprisingly, the work breakdown structure and the macro plan each require a number of activities to be completed before they can be produced.

THE MACRO PLAN

Macro plans vary in length depending on the size of the project. The first draft of a plan can often be substantial, perhaps as large as 50 pages in length. This is too large, and the author, in this instance the project manager, needs to reduce the plan in size. An average length for an advanced project is between 3,000 and 6,000 words. Keeping the plan to this length makes it quick to read and also forces you to be succinct. This is important since the principal readership of the macro plan will be senior executives. These executives will have little time available and so will want to be able to understand the macro plan for the project quickly.

A well-written macro plan presents its reader with an overview of the project, enabling them to grasp its fundamental purpose and its objectives. It should explain how you, as project manager, will deal with the foundation aspects of the project effectively and what risks will be involved. There are three foundation aspects you need to consider:

1. timescale;
2. scope;
3. quality.

Timescale and scope

Generally, those interested in the outcome of the project focus on two areas, timescale and scope. This can prove to be very challenging. It is difficult to set timescales without knowing the scope, and difficult to set the scope without understanding the timescales. To overcome this, the project manager should pick on one area and focus attention on it. Once a reasonable definition has been achieved, the project manager can then return to the other area. Generally, timescale should be tackled first since this is often the driving force behind the business case. It is also normally the question that is posed most often to the project manager: 'When will the project be ready?'

Ideally you would be able to spend a significant amount of time working through the project requirements. As you completed the work you would feel able to produce estimates for timescales and task scope. Ultimately this would yield a plan which you would feel happy committing to. However, events rarely happen in this manner in advanced projects. Senior managers and directors are keen to set timescales early in the planning process. They want to see rapid progress and view the setting of timescales as an important milestone in that progress.

Inexperienced project managers find this part of the project process very difficult. They are in charge of a large and usually difficult project that is being carefully scrutinized by senior managers. These are the same senior managers who will help shape the project manager's future career. For project managers, this situation can be very challenging. They can and unfortunately often do fail at this stage. They fight senior managers for more time and in doing so they do significant damage to important relationships. Senior managers become disillusioned with the project manager and often this culminates with the project manager being replaced. Avoiding this is surprisingly easy. You should work initially with target timescales rather than estimated timescales. This will enable you to avoid potential conflicts with senior managers.

For inexperienced project managers, working with target timescales can prove to be uncomfortable. They are concerned that even discussing the targets might lead senior managers into expecting something that will ultimately not be delivered. They're worried that the timescales resulting from the estimation process will be significantly different from the target timescales and that they will be unable to explain the differences satisfactorily. The key to overcoming this is to effectively manage senior managers' expectations.

Setting senior managers' expectations and setting a basic time line

The first action you should take is to define what timescales are being requested by senior managers. This should not include any

Senior Manager Interview Form				
Name of interviewee: **Reference number:** SMI/XXX/YYY **Date:** DD/MM/YY				
Questions				
What would be a successful outcome for you?				
What would be a successful outcome for the organization?				
What would be a successful outcome for the project team?				
What specific deliverables would you like to see?				
What specific deliverables do you think the organization might want additionally?				
When would you like to see these deliverables?				
How would you measure whether these deliverables have been successfully achieved?				
What if any interim stages do you see in producing the deliverables?				
What level of resources do you believe should be applied to the production of the deliverables?				
Wish list				
Description	Ideal delivery date	Measurement of success	Interim delivery suggestion	Resource levels expected
Approvals				

Figure 2.1 Interview template

type of scope or feasibility assessment. You should simply seek to understand what senior managers would like to achieve and when they would like to achieve it by. Effectively you should be seeking the wish list of senior managers. This can be achieved easily by interviewing the key senior managers and asking them what their ideal project outcome would be. To ensure consistency throughout the interviewing process it is helpful if you use a standard form. A sample form is shown in Figure 2.1.

The form contains nine questions whose objective is to guide you through the general areas that should be covered. It is simple to add more questions to the form to cover the specific issues that are relevant to the project. However, before doing this you should consider whether there will be time available during the interview to capture more specific information. Most interviews will be one hour or less in duration. This gives you about five minutes a question (based on the template form) with a few minutes to cover introductions, getting coffee, etc. Practically this means that if you want to add questions then you probably need to remove the equivalent number of questions from the standard form. If you feel that you do want to remove questions then you should be careful in their substitution.

None of the questions in the standard form are very specific. This is achieved through careful design. They are designed to ensure that the interviewee is encouraged to talk. The assumption behind the questions is one of listening and understanding. It is worth remembering that this is not formal requirements capture. This activity is designed to enable you to gain a general understanding of what is desired by senior managers. Questions like 'What should the colour of the building be?' or 'What should the user interface on the program look like?' won't help you to gain that understanding.

Once the basic ideas have been captured they should be put together in a list. This list then forms the initial baseline that you should work towards. You should pass a copy of the completed form and the associated wish list back to the senior manager concerned to allow the manager to correct misinterpretations.

When all of the key senior managers have contributed to the wish list you should publish a final list. This list should be passed to all of the people interviewed, which should include all the members of the project steering group. When this list is published you will have accomplished an important milestone. For the first time you will be able to state publicly the key objectives of the project including the target time line. Importantly, you will be able to back the statement with support from the organization's principal project sponsors. The next stage is to refine and develop that list into a high-level target plan. This is the start of the formal requirements capture process.

Capturing the requirements

Many organizations have departments who are dedicated to defining and capturing requirements. Other organizations operate on an ad hoc basis, setting up meetings on an 'as needed' basis. In both types of organization you will need to take on a coordinating role. In an organization where a requirements department is available this role will be much simpler. However, as with many other areas of advanced projects it is unlikely that the department will have processes set up specifically to cover advanced projects.

When an organization does not have a requirements capture department you will need to lead the process yourself. One of the simplest but most effective ways of capturing requirements is the use of brainstorming sessions. There are many different brainstorming techniques available and many consultancies happy to run sessions for organizations unsure of the process. Whilst external parties can add significant value it is probably sufficient at this stage to run the session using in-house resources. Later, once the direction is clearer, external help could be sought.

Running a brainstorming session is something that you should be capable of. It is a key technique that will be used repeatedly in various forms throughout the course of the project. The technique described below is simple. This makes it easy for participants in the session to understand their role and what is expected of them. This helps to ensure that they are concentrating on the outcome of the session rather than the methodology that the brainstorm session is using. Participants focused in this way normally are able to produce good results that centre on the question being asked.

- *Step 1*
  Prior to the meeting you should send each participant a copy of the senior management wish list. You should also send them a copy of the brainstorming technique explanation sheet included on the CD ROM.

  At the start of the session you should gather all the participants together and explain how the brainstorming session will work. You should explain that at the end of the session you would like to have gathered a high-level task list. This task list should enable the project to produce a plan that will deliver the senior managers' wish list. Therefore you require:
  - a proposed task;
  - timescale for the task;
  - likely cost for the task, in terms of people and equipment.
  It is worth while reassuring the participants that it might not be possible to cover the whole project in one brainstorm session. You should explain that if this happens then you will arrange a further session to enable the brainstorm to be completed.
- *Step 2*
  Give each person a small pad of paper and a thick marker pen. Ideally each person should have their own identifiable colour. You should ask everyone to write one requirement per page on the writing pad they've been given. Each idea should be expressed in a few words. Participants can use as many or as few pages as they wish. However, they should write down all of the high-level or overview requirements that they can think of.

  This process should be allowed to continue for between 10 and 15 minutes. This is usually long enough for the brainstorm meeting participants to run out of ideas. Participants are allowed to write anything on the pads of paper. Ideas can

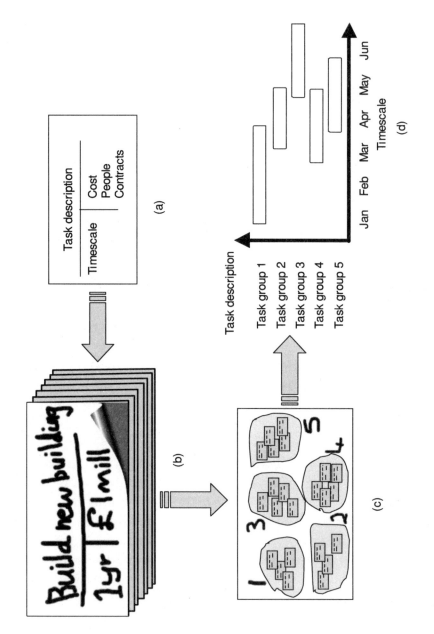

Figure 2.2 Target plan creation

include process, timescale, costs, risks, people issues and of course scope.

- *Step 3*
  When participants have exhausted their ideas, ask them to stick the individual pages on to a designated wall. This can be done with tape or sticky tack. Ideally, pads with sticky backs should be used. The ideas can be placed anywhere on the wall although it will speed up the process if like ideas are grouped together.
- *Step 4*
  After all the notes have been placed on the wall you should ask one or two members of the group to sift through the pages and order them into groups of like ideas. Now the wall should be covered with a series of groups. Some of the groups may only have one member.
- *Step 5*
  Once the sorting is complete the team should collectively audit the grouped ideas. Whilst doing this the group should ensure that they understand the ideas by questioning the author. Often this will result in the addition of timescales and resource requirements. The participants should ensure that the pages are grouped in a manner that all of the attendees agree with. They should add a name for each task grouping.
- *Step 6*
  You (or someone nominated by the brainstorm team) should gather together the groups of ideas and translate them into a form that explains the rationale behind them. This should be done outside of the brainstorm session. You should now have a list that outlines a series of high-level requirements. This should include both the task to be completed and the target timescale for its completion. You should now send the output to the brainstorm meeting participants for comment and review.

The whole process is shown diagrammatically in Figure 2.2. Initially, a template, Figure 2.2(a), is given for the capture of the various tasks that will need to be completed. These are then written on pads of paper, Figure 2.2(b), and then the papers are grouped together on a wall, Figure 2.2(c). Finally the task groups are translated into a simple schedule, Figure 2.2(d).

It is worth remembering that at this stage the requirements will be written in their simplest form. Detailing them will happen during the next phase of the project when the detailed plan is produced.

The simplicity of this technique masks the underlying expectation management. It tackles this in three ways. Firstly, it ensures that ideas are captured in the words of the author. No idea is perceived to have been changed in the capture process. Secondly, all of the voices in the group are heard. The ideas from the less vocal members of the group are as visible as those of the more forceful members. Thirdly, everyone feels that their idea has added value to the process since it ultimately contributes to one of the final task groupings.

If the work was carried out by an internal requirements capture department there should be a similar list to the one produced by the brainstorm session. Whichever list is available it should provide a series of tasks and associated timescales. It should now be translated into a simple schedule and published to a wider audience for comment. When resource or quality requirements have been identified these should be included with any material sent out for comment. The audience should include any technical authorities within the organization or other groups that may be involved in successfully delivering the project. The recipients should be asked to consider the proposed timescales, the desired scope and the associated risks. Their remit is to check whether the schedule can be developed into a reasonable plan. The plan sent out for review should look something like the one shown in Figure 2.2(d).

This is only a sample plan and you should expect that your plan will have more activities. The number will be defined by the number of task groups resulting from your brainstorming session. You should, however, consider carefully the needs of the audience of this plan. There are likely to be two types of reader: firstly, senior managers who want a high level understanding of the project and, secondly, more junior managers who want a more detailed understanding of the project.

The senior managers need a one-page picture of the key events that will happen over the project lifetime. This means that if your current set of task groups won't fit on to one page you should consider combining some of them. For example, you could set task group 1 as the initial design specification, task group 2 as the building of the new building, task group 3 as the fit-out of the new building, task group 4 as the transfer of staff and task group 5 as the commissioning of the building.

The more junior managers will be interested in the one-page picture as well but they will also need the explanatory notes. You should produce these notes in accordance with your interpretation of the brainstorm session. They should enable the reader to begin to understand what is being sought and enable them to make a better judgement about scope feasibility. It is also helpful to supply these managers with a copy of the initial senior managers' wish lists.

Although it is possible that you could gain agreement to this outline plan by simply sending it out for comment, it is unlikely. Instead to enable you to reach a plan that is accepted by the various stakeholders you should set up a review schedule. This schedule should set out the timing of several review iterations. Each of the iterations should include some time for comment and then some time for upgrading the document prior to it being sent out for further comment. For an advanced project you should plan on between three and five iterations. You should encourage iterations to happen quickly. Those involved in the review should be encouraged to adopt a best-guess approach; accuracy will come later.

Each round of commenting will result in more detail being added to the overall plan. This will mean that a deeper understanding of each task grouping will be developed. You should be able to develop a schedule that represents each task grouping leaving you with a more detailed plan at the end of the iterations. This plan should be sufficient to allow the initial planning and estimation of resources, which is the next stage in the development of the macro plan development.

Estimating the resources

The planning and estimation of resources should, where possible, be undertaken by the line units that will carry out the work. Ideally these units will have experience of similar work in previous projects. This experience will help to improve the accuracy of the developing plan. Working in this manner also helps to ensure that the units have the opportunity to influence the work. This helps the units to feel part of the overall project and ultimately part of the team.

At this stage the purpose of estimation is to gain a high-level assessment rather than an accurate detailed plan. As a result, those estimating should be encouraged to be quick and coarse in their estimation. To help those estimating, a simple estimating technique should be used. Those estimating resource levels should be sent the form shown in Table 2.1 to complete and return.

There are two main types of estimators, those with a pessimistic view and those with an optimistic view. When estimating tasks,

Table 2.1 Estimation form for task groups

Task group description (eg task group 1)	Analogy	Best case	Most likely	Worst case
Headcount				
Other cost				

Analogy code: DB – done this or similar before
RS – done something reasonably similar before
ND – not done before

people generally fall into one of these two categories. The form is designed to overcome these natural tendencies, by enabling estimators to put down a range of estimates. Estimators are also asked to include an analogy assessment in addition to the three-point estimate: best case, most likely case and worst case.

An analogy estimate is simply a method of estimating based on previous or historical data or experience. Analogy data are very important for the project manager. It is the analogy assessment that enables you to make a judgement about which estimate to use. For example, if the analogy is DB (done before) then you can with a degree of confidence use the most likely estimates. Conversely if the analogy is NB (not done before) then you might choose the worst case estimates. This is the simplest approach to picking which estimate to use.

A more comprehensive approach can be achieved by determining the nature of the estimators. The easiest example is for estimates classed DB. If the task has been done before then the range given should be small or non-existent. So if the estimator has given a large range then it's reasonable to assume that the estimator is highly cautious in nature. However, care needs to be taken not to assume that the opposite is true. If the class is DB and the range small then this doesn't mean that the estimator is optimistic; it's more likely that the estimator is realistic. To discover optimistic estimators, the ND classification should be examined. If the range is small then it's likely that the estimator is being optimistic.

Armed with the estimates and knowing the nature of the estimators, you are now able to build the first draft of the project plan. This plan will still be a best-guess plan but the estimation technique and the process to get to this point mean that the plan is likely to be a reasonable representation of the final plan. Once you have completed the first draft of the plan you should send it to the various team members involved so far, for review, comment and in due course agreement.

You should treat this plan in a similar manner to the requirements that you generated previously. This means that you should set up an iterative review whose objective is getting the plan agreed.

Once the estimated plan and the requirements have been completed and agreed two additional parts need to be added to complete the macro plan: a quality statement for each task group and a high-level resource plan.

Quality statement

In advanced projects, planning quality in at the start is often overlooked or deliberately ignored. This is a mistake. Including a quality statement at this stage is simple and will result in the project being able to reap ongoing benefits. Describing quality does not have to be an onerous task. Instead simply defining a quality objective against each of the task groups is enough. This objective should be focused on setting out how the project should measure whether the task concerned has been successfully completed. An example of a task with a quality statement embedded might be: 'A building should last a minimum of 20 years and require no maintenance for 10 years.'

Often project managers produce a large plan quoting the company quality manual standards. However, a simple table works just as well. The table allows you to set out clearly the known tasks against the quality goals. Where a task group has been subdivided into several activities, each activity should be given a quality objective.

Once the quality objectives have been defined it is worth while reviewing the plan to ensure that it still is achievable. You should review with each of the estimators the impact that the quality objectives might have on the estimates that they provided. They should check whether the estimates are still valid given the assumptions they made or whether a further revision is needed. If a further revision is made then the revised plan should be sent back out for review and agreement.

You should now be in a position to release a macro plan. This should be a combination of the high-level requirements from the brainstorming and the task estimates. This plan can now be used as the basis for generating other material prior to the preparation of the final business case.

BUDGET

Once you have completed the macro plan the next step is to produce a budget for the project. At this stage this means producing a coarse budget with an accompanying sensitivity analysis.

The budget plan is often thought of as the budget statement and it is based on the task, resource and timescale estimates that were previously completed to enable the production of the macro plan. As with the task estimating, the objective is to produce a coarse estimate rather than a very accurate estimate. This enables you to go quickly and present the budget for approval in principle sooner.

Building a project budget is a mechanistic task. However, it does demand a methodical and thorough approach from you or whoever will be responsible for its production. Trying to cut corners to speed the process up will normally result in disaster.

The first step is to work out all the relevant costs that can be associated with the tasks defined so far. The identified costs should be split into capital and revenue costs. Capital costs are those that occur on a once-off basis – for example buying a software program. Revenue costs are those that occur on an ongoing basis – for example the maintenance of the software program.

Normally the largest revenue cost for a project is the staff cost. Calculating this cost first helps to put the other revenue costs into perspective. If they are less than 1 per cent of the staff costs it is not worth spending a significant amount of time calculating them. To make the cost calculation easier it is useful to set up a spreadsheet. A sample spreadsheet is shown in Table 2.2.

Most of the information required to populate the table will already have been gathered. It is likely that for any given task

Table 2.2 Task group revenue cost calculation

| Task group description | Name | Resource cost | | | |
		Headcount	Days	Unit cost	Subtotal
Task group 1	John Smith	10	10	£200	£20,000
Task group 1	Susan Kell	20	20	£600	£240,000
Task group 2	Robin Saks	15	15	£400	£90,000
Task group 3	John Lost	6	6	£250	£9,000
Task group 4	Wun Torn	12	12	£525	£75,600

Headcount from analogy estimate (see Table 2.1)   Duration of task from target plan (see Figure 2.2)   Unit cost from internal accounts

there will be more than one person working. This is shown in Table 2.2 for task group 1. By simply inserting an extra line in the table you can easily add resources. This method can also be applied for people who are working for the same length of time but have different unit costs.

In addition to identifying the task-based costs you must also identify the capital costs for the project. This should also be done on a task-by-task basis. At this early project stage it is likely that many of the capital costs will be unknown and as a result the costs will be best guesses. A simple way to improve the guess of the cost is to use a three-point estimation technique. This is simply a repetition of the method used earlier for estimating task resource needs. A sample table is shown in Table 2.3.

You need to judge which costs you should use. So as with the resource estimates you should assess the estimators using the analogy criteria. With an assessment of the estimators you should be able to determine which costs to use. Once you have determined the costs you should collate them with the resource costs into a table like the one shown in Table 2.4.

Table 2.3 Capital cost estimation

Cost description	Analogy	Best case	Most likely	Worst case
Total				

Analogy code: DB – done this or similar before
RS   – done something reasonably similar before
ND – not done before

The table shows a month-by-month timescale. This timescale was arbitrarily chosen and should be changed to fit with the overall length of the actual project concerned. In most cases months will be the minimum time period that should be used. It is more likely that quarterly or six-month periods will be appropriate for an

Table 2.4 Task costs consolidation

	Jan		Feb		Mar		Apr		May		Jun		Jul		Total
Task description	R	C	R	C	R	C	R	C	R	C	R	C	R	C	
Total															

R – revenue   C – capital

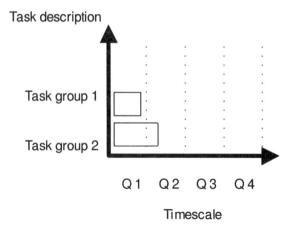

Figure 2.3 Distributing the costs

advanced project. Each time slot is split into two parts, the revenue costs and the capital costs. These costs are totalled at the bottom of the columns. This total is then the total expenditure per month or per quarter depending on the time period used.

Once the costs have been attributed across the various months it is likely that there will be cost scheduling issues. This is illustrated in Figure 2.3.

Figure 2.3 shows two tasks. The costs associated with the first task are all contained in the first quarter. However the second task, task group 2, is split across quarter 1 and quarter 2. You need to decide whether the cost gets written up in the first quarter, the second quarter or apportioned between the quarters.

The simplest way of dealing with the cost is to attribute it on a straight-line or linear basis. This is achieved by dividing the total cost for task group 2, by 4, the period over which the task runs. If the total cost for task group 2 is £40,000 then this means that £10,000 is spent per month for four consecutive months. This means that £30,000 is attributed to the first quarter and £10,000 is attributed to the second quarter. In most cases this method is sufficient. However, in some cases it is necessary to model the cost for the task.

Modelling costs can be complicated. However, at this stage simplicity is always better since the planning is still at a coarse

Table 2.5 Financial profile

	Quarter				
Cost description	1	2	3	4	Total
Linear costs					
Modelled costs					
Total					

level. Modelling costs should only be used when the cost is obviously not spent in a linear manner, for example when there is a large payment due at the start of the task perhaps as part of contract signing. As the planning progresses, more and more sophisticated models can be used. It is likely that you will have both linear and modelled costs. These should be added together and put into a table like the one shown in Table 2.5.

This table shows the total costs per quarter for the project. This shows the total spend that the project requires to make in the given time period and therefore the amount of funding the organization needs to supply, a key ingredient for the business case.

Contingency

Before finalizing the budget, additional cost should be added for contingency. Contingency is the addition of funds to the project budget to allow for tasks becoming more expensive than originally planned. This can occur where project tasks run late or where they are underestimated or the external supplier costs more than expected.

One method of calculating contingency is to assume that all costs used in the budget preparation are the most likely costs. This then allows a mechanistic method of calculating the contingency on a task-by-task basis. This is achieved simply by: 1 - (best case/ worst case) × best case. The sum of this calculated cost and the

Best Case	Worst Case	% Difference	Contingency	Final Funds
£10,000	£20,000	50%	£5,000	£15,000
£15,000	£16,000	6%	£938	£15,938
£1,000	£6,000	83%	£833	£1,833
£2,000	£7,000	71%	£1,429	£3,429
£3,000	£8,000	63%	£1,875	£4,875

Figure 2.4(a) Contingency calculation

most likely cost is the contingency-adjusted figure. This figure accounts for the difference between the best case and worst case scenarios. This is illustrated in Figure 2.4.

The table in Figure 2.4(a) shows that a large difference between best and worst case returns a high contingency. Conversely when the difference between the best case and worst case is low the contingency figure is lower. This can be illustrated by the curve in Figure 2.4(b). In the figure the initial slope of the curve is steep and the end of the curve is shallow. Effectively the calculated result is normally close to the most likely figure for the work. This means that excessive amounts of contingency are not added unless the worst case and best case estimates vary enormously.

The main difficulty with using this method for calculating contingency is its reliance on the use of the best case estimate. It is really only appropriate to use this when the task estimate is based on or close to the best case or most likely case estimate. Often project managers will use worst case figures where they believe the task risk is high. In these cases the calculation for contingency will not work.

An alternative method of calculating contingency is simply to add a 5 per cent or 10 per cent allowance on top of the total project budget requirement. This pragmatic approach often produces a very similar result to the more technical and mechanist approach.

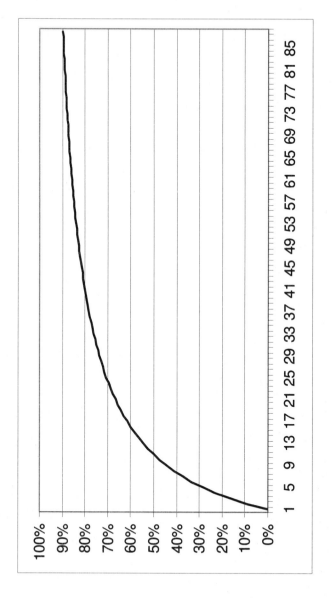

Figure 2.4(b) Contingency weight attribution

Reserve

As well as adding contingency to the budget you should also add a project reserve. Reserve funds are included for coping with forgotten areas of spend. The amount you should set aside depends greatly on the type of the project that you are managing. If it is a completely new project and the work is unknown then setting aside a very large reserve is advisable. Projects such as the Channel tunnel or the baggage handling system at Denver airport both overran their initial budgets by more than 100 per cent.

If it is a project that is similar to one undertaken before then the amount set aside should be a lot less. In some cases it is acceptable not to set aside any funds. Instead anything that is forgotten is sought from the organization's normal operating funds. It should now be possible to construct a final budget. The final budget consists of the calculated cost for revenue and capital, the contingency cost and the reserve cost.

Once the budget is complete you should be able to start producing the business case for the project. You should now have all of the information necessary to enable you to pull together a compelling business case.

Business case production

Leaving the approval of the business case until this point in the planning can make project managers uncomfortable. Many project managers would hope to write and get approved their business case at the start of the project. However, business cases approved early on in the project life cycle often are only approved in principle and generally they need to be continually revisited as the project progresses.

Leaving the production of the business case until this stage in the project enables you to use the information developed so far in the business case material. This material is built on firm ground and will have been worked through with the steering group. Practically this means that the steering group members will be happier to approve the business case fully.

The style and format for the business case will vary from organization to organization. Whenever possible you should use the organization's style, thereby avoiding duplication of existing work. However, regardless of the template, in almost all organizations two basic questions will remain at the heart of the business case: 1) What is going to be done? 2) What is the commercial justification for doing it?

What is going to be done?

Writing the first part of the business case is something that either you or the project sponsor should undertake. Writing this part of the business case should be relatively straightforward since all of the information needed is already available from the macro plan. This presents the requirements and timescales in a coherent fashion and it is often called the 'project strategy'. Many organizations will have a prescribed format for this part of the business case. However, as with many areas of work in advanced projects it is also likely that no template will be available. When this happens you should adopt a simple format.

The first area to present is a written summary of the project's aims and objectives. This should concentrate on the commercial value of the completion of the project. If you are writing the material you should present it in an overview manner. The presentation should explain what will be done, why it is commercially justified and how much it will cost. This should be between 200 and 400 words in length. If the project cannot be summarized in this volume of words then the project is not properly understood. Skilled project managers should always be able to summarize their project simply – they will have to do this many times as the project progresses.

Once the initial summary is written then the second area to include is a presentation of the scope of the project. It is not necessary to present all of the tasks from the brainstorm meeting or the senior managers' wish lists. Whilst this material is relevant it should be relegated to an appendix to the plan. What should be presented is the main task groups and, in detail, a description of any task that you consider to be high-risk. You can identify high-risk tasks from the analogy estimation carried out as part of the task and cost estimations. The high-risk tasks are those that have been identified as not done (ND) before.

What is the commercial justification for doing it?

Once you or the project sponsor have written the scope section of the business case you need to produce part two, the commercial justification. Producing the commercial justification is normally the project sponsor's responsibility. However, the majority of the work on this area will have been completed either by you or by the finance department. As a result, the project sponsor will need significant help in producing this section of the business case.

Normally the commercial justification presents the proposed cost estimates for the project and accompanies them with a project revenue stream that will result at the completion of the project. This enables a cash flow to be determined and an investment decision made. The cash flow and the investment part are normally dealt with by the finance part of the organization rather than the project.

The project normally presents the cost basis for the project. It can be tempting to present the costs using a copy of the tables already developed (eg the cash flow). This should be avoided. The purpose of the presentation is to give an overview of the costs, not a detailed account of them. As with the task summary, the detail should be presented in an appendix. The best way to present the resource and budget requirements of the project is to start from the broadest level. This means saying the project will take x years and cost between £y and £z. Many project managers leave this statement until the end of the justification. They feel the correct way to present the cost is to build up to this statement rather than state it at the start. They are wrong. Stating the overall cost in the opening section is the right way of managing the readers. If you do not do this, the first thing readers will do is flip forward until they find the figures that they are looking for. By building from the top down, readers are encouraged to build understanding. The simplest way to validate this approach is to consider what you would say if someone told you figures in this way. A general format would be:

The project will take x months to complete and will require between £z and £v in funding.

£z is the lower-risk estimate and is calculated on the lowest resource and capital expenditure estimates. See Appendix Z.

£v is the higher-risk estimate and is calculated on the highest resource and capital expenditure estimates. See Appendix Z.

The tasks with the widest cost range are:

X	min cost	max cost
Y	min cost	max cost

Business case approval

Once the business case is complete the next step is to seek formal approval for its implementation. Surprisingly it is not always clear who has the approval authority for an advanced project's business case. This applies equally to organizations that have properly documented procedures and those that do not have them. Advanced projects are not like other projects. Organizations do not undertake many of them in the course of a year. Often they involve a complicated move in strategy for the organization, something that does not happen particularly often. The small frequency of occurrence means that procedures to cover the eventuality are often not produced. Where there is a lack of process you need to rely on the steering group that you have already formed. You should seek approval from them for the business case and the associated plans.

It is likely that your steering group will already include a director or someone very senior in the organization. When you take the business case forward you should also ensure that you have added any technical and business authorities. You should also assess if there is another project relying on the use of the same resources as your project. If there is then that project manager should also be invited. This serves two purposes. Firstly, it ensures that any conflict is brought into the open where it can be dealt with effectively. Secondly, it's always good practice to have another peer review the plans that you have produced. Hopefully, the other person can add value by suggesting areas for improvement.

Often the approval meeting can become long and tedious. Participants get weary and the result is a very poor start for the project. This should be avoided. You should prepare the approval session well in advance. The simplest way to do this is to brief the proposed attendees before the meeting. This should be on a one-to-one basis and it should give you an opportunity to understand any potential disagreements that might exist. It is also an opportunity for finding and developing possible solutions that would be acceptable.

Once all the members of the steering group have been canvassed for their views in one-to-one meetings then the business case should be updated. This updated version of the plan should take account of difficulties or problems found and it should be sent out to the steering group members. Once the members have had a short time to review the material the steering group should meet to review the business case for approval. At the meeting the business case should be presented. This presentation should include a commentary of the key issues and their proposed solutions.

If it is difficult to carry out one-to-one reviews then an alternative is to use a paper review. A paper review involves sending to each of the steering group meeting participants the macro plan and a comment sheet. The comment sheets are gathered together and analysed, and the document is iterated. After several iterations the business case is normally pretty complete and the steering group can be called together.

It is worth sounding a note of caution about this approach. Whilst this might seem an attractive approach it does prove to be less focused and less fruitful than one-to-one meetings. Reviewers comment on the quality of the English rather than the substance of the document. It is only when they get to the meeting that they start really to discuss the essence of the business case.

Whatever method is chosen, the purpose of the review is to get the organization behind the project. This is the sole objective that you should have in mind when running the meeting. Project managers often find it difficult to remain dispassionate about their projects. They want to argue down dissenting voices, not promote them into being considered. However, it is much better to hear and deal publicly with the views than to have them aired privately behind your back. Your role is to ensure that all points of view are heard and dealt with effectively – even the negative ones!

THE WORK BREAKDOWN STRUCTURE

Once the business case has been approved, it is important for the project manager to move quickly on to the development of the work breakdown structure. The work breakdown structure is the structure that all project work is set against. It takes the existing plans and breaks them into manageable groups of work. For example, developing a software package might be broken into development, testing, project management and requirements management. There are many ways to define the work breakdown structure for a project but the method explained here normally proves effective.

To transform the existing plans into a work breakdown structure you need to use the schedule (or Gantt chart) developed as part of the macro plan. The schedule is likely to appear like a much larger version of the one shown in Figure 2.5.

The first step in changing this schedule into a work breakdown structure is rotating the schedule by 90 degrees. This is shown in Figure 2.6.

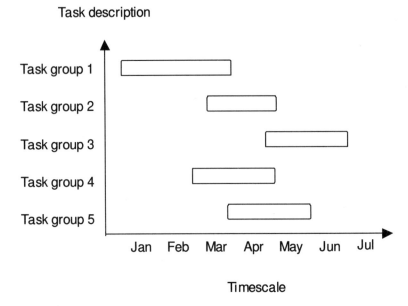

Figure 2.5 Macro plan

The chart can now be interpreted as showing five potential work packages, task group 5 running from March till May to task group 1 running from January to April. With a simple chart like this one it seems obvious that each of the task groups should be managed as a separate work package. However, a full plan for a real project would have many more task groups than five. When this happens it makes sense to group tasks together. There are several possible reasons for combing task groups together into a single work package:

- time;
- resource;
- similar work content.

Time

In general, projects run to a given life cycle like the one shown in Figure 2.7. This shows the general work flow that a project will

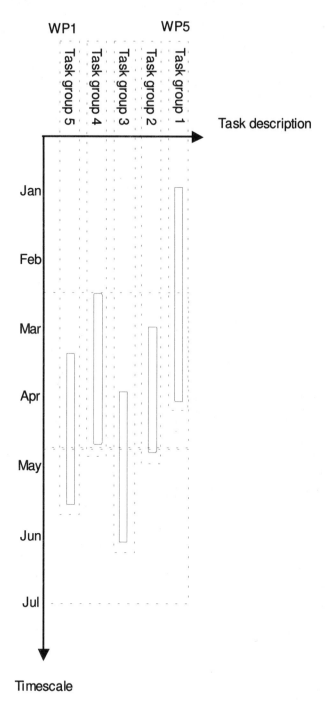

Figure 2.6 WBS – first pass

follow is: requirements work, development work, testing work and finally release work. The curves related to each phase depict the amount of effort that is expended by the project team on an activity at any given moment in time. At the start of the project the majority of the work is focused on requirements. This focus rapidly changes into a focus on development work. This shift in attention happens since the project team will start to work on implementing requirements as soon as they are agreed. They do not wait for all the requirements to be completed before they start work on implementation. Similarly with the testing phase, the testers do not wait for all the development to complete before starting their work. Instead they begin planning as soon as is practicable. As the testing phase completes, the final stage, the release phase, starts. The end of the release phase is the end of the project.

Knowing that the work in a project occurs in this manner allows the project manager to consider grouping tasks solely on the basis of where they occur in time. If task groups occur at the start of a project then it is likely that they are involved in requirements capture. If they occur at the end it is likely that they are related to the testing or release phases.

Returning to Figure 2.6 and examining it in this way reveals that task group 2 and task group 4 are related in time. Both have similar timescales for completion. It is therefore likely that the work they will be performing will be related. Therefore it would be worth considering joining these two task groups together to form one work package.

Using the time-based approach to forming work packages enables project managers to focus on the current work because the current work will be grouped together in the same work package. If project managers keep the number of work packages small, between six and eight in total, then they will only have to focus on one or two work packages at any moment in time. So using the time-based approach ensures that project managers are able to spend significant time on the current work. They will not be in the position of worrying about other work not receiving sufficient attention.

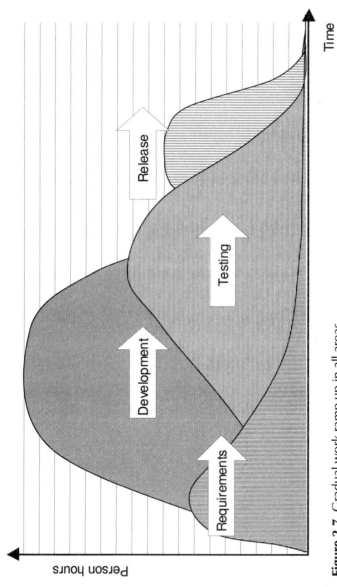

Figure 2.7 Gradual work ramp-up in all areas

Resource

Although the time-based approach to setting up a work package has advantages, it also has difficulties. The principal difficulty arises because tasks are all different in size and volume of work. In Figure 2.6 it is possible that task group 2 and task group 4 may be double the size of all the other tasks. This can be seen visually in Figure 2.8, which relates Figure 2.6 to Figure 2.7.

Task group 1 seems likely to be the activity associated with the requirements phase. Task group 2 and task group 4 seem likely to be the activities associated with the development phase. Task group 5 seems likely to be the testing phase activities and task group 3 the release phase activities. If this is the correct interpretation then task group 2 and task group 4 are likely to account for the majority of the volume of work. This makes it less sensible to merge the two task groups into one work package. It would be more sensible to spread the resources evenly across all of the work packages. Levelling the resources in the work packages helps to reduce the number of management levels needed for successful control. Reducing the number of levels in turn reduces the risk of failure. To overcome this difficulty in setting up work packages, some method of levelling the volume of work across the proposed work packages needs to be used.

To level the volume of work on its own is not a difficult task. The project manager should first set up the work packages by the time-based method previously explained. Once this is complete each work package should be examined in relation to the amount of resource being applied to it. Where a work package is grossly different to the other work packages then the project manager should consider splitting it into two work packages.

In addition to examining work packages for over-allocation of resource volumes, the project manager should examine them for under-allocation of resource volumes. A sample table of potential resource volumes for five work packages is shown in Figure 2.9.

Joining task group 2 and task group 4 would not be sensible for the scenario shown in Figure 2.9. Joining them would create a

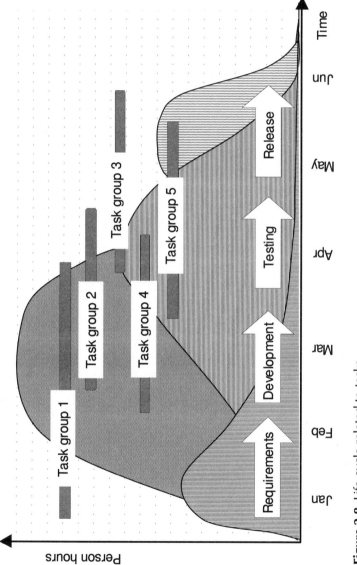

Figure 2.8 Life cycle related to tasks

Task Group	Resource (Heads)
TG 1	1
TG 2	30
TG 3	10
TG 4	50
TG 5	7

Work Package	Resource Required
1: TG 1	1 head
2: TG 2 + TG 4	30 + 50 = 80 heads
3: TG 3	10 heads
4: TG 5	7 heads

Figure 2.9 Work package resource levels

very large work package in relation to the other proposed work packages. Neither would it be sensible to have separate work packages for task groups 1, 3 and 5 since the resultant work packages would be under-allocated. Instead to avoid the over-allocation (joining task groups 2 and 4) and under-allocation (single work packages for task groups 1, 3 and 5) it would be more reasonable to create three work packages: one work package that combines task groups 1, 3 and 5, one work package for task group 2 and one work package for task group 4.

Similar work content

Deciding on work packages only on the basis of position in time and volume of resources fails to account for the work content of the task grouping. In many cases this will not pose a problem since the natural life cycle of the project will ensure that like activities are grouped together. However, problems can and do arise. The final work package configuration for the case considered above joined together three work packages on the basis of their resource levels. However, a different combination could have been achieved that might have ensured a smoother project.

Joining task group 1 and task group 2 (or alternatively task group 1 and task group 4) would have allowed the creation of a work package that is more likely to have similar work activity. Both task group 2 and task group 4 occur at the start of the project along with the end of task group 1. All are likely to be involved in requirements work. Where this similarity of activity can be achieved, it helps to reduce the risk of project failure. A common goal in relation to work activity ensures that resources are more likely to be able to support one another should something go wrong. Similarly, at the other end of the timescale it would perhaps be more sensible to join task groups 3 and 5 together.

Once project managers have assessed the project task groups from the three different perspectives they should be in a position to produce a draft work breakdown structure. The work breakdown structure is normally drawn as shown in Figure 2.10.

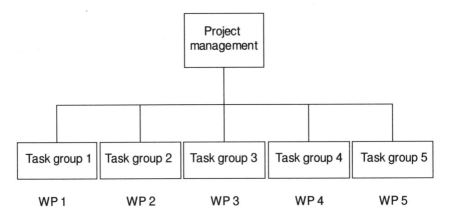

Figure 2.10 WBS outline

Although this diagram shows the work packages as discrete areas of work, they should not be thought of in this manner. It is important to remember that each of the work packages is related to the others. This is clearly illustrated by Figure 2.8, which shows the overlapping nature of the work in each phase. For example, task group 3 is the release activity and task group 5 the testing activity. Clearly task group 3 needs to start whilst task group 5 is in progress if unnecessary delay is to be avoided. You need to remember this when developing the detailed levels of the work breakdown structure.

WORK PACKAGE DETAILED PLANNING

Once the work package structure has been designed, the next stage is to develop the detail of the individual work packages. The first stage in development is the appointment of a suitable work package manager. This is the person who will manage the work package on a day-to-day basis. The work package manager will be responsible for ensuring delivery of the work package and for marshalling the resources within it. Work package managers are usually fairly easy to identify within organizations. They are normally senior managers whose area of work significantly overlaps with the work content of the work package.

Many organizations have standard processes for work package development and where these exist they should be completed as directed. If there is not a standard work package template then you should design one. A template that could be used as the basis for the design is shown in the table in Figure 2.11.

Work package:						Revision: XX			
Work package ID: X.X						Date: DD/MM/YY			
Work package owner: Joe Smith									
Description									
Deliverables									
Key risks									
Resources required					Funds required				
Type	Q1	Q2	Q3	Q4	Type	Q1	Q2	Q3	Q4
Quality goals									
Delegated boundaries									
Sign-off									
Resource owner --									
Project manager --									
Work package manager --									

Figure 2.11 Work package detailed description

The form shows the areas that you must consider when designing each work package: cost, quality, resource and scope. Although the form is self-explanatory, there are two sections that are worth special attention: delegated boundaries and sign-off.

Boundaries

Work package managers can be delegated significant authority. Ensuring that the delegated authority and its associated boundaries are clearly agreed between you and the work package manager is very important. Sadly, this clear agreement is not always achieved. Instead understanding is confined to being a by-product of the discussions covering the scope and content of the work package. Agreement is never achieved in this manner and relationships become strained when this method is adopted. It is essential that you discuss this section properly with the work package manager. Authority to act when properly delegated can be one of the most powerful ways of motivating staff, and motivated staff make the project more likely to succeed.

Completing this section is not simply achieved by setting the boundaries and then adding suitable text to the boundaries section of the form. Instead it is essential that you use the box as a mechanism for discussion with the work package manager about suitable boundaries. The discussion should be initiated and driven by you. You should continue to drive the discussion until an acceptable agreement has been reached. You should ensure that the discussion covers:

- resource and its deployment;
- interfaces and their associated responsibilities;
- capital and funds expenditure;
- use of contingency and reserve;
- change control and its management;
- reporting and levels of control.

To achieve a successful result it is helpful if prior to the meeting you assess each of these areas. This should result in you producing a list of points for each area of discussion. At the meeting you should allow the work package manager to lead the discussion. You should only take the lead if a point you have on your list is missed out. This way of working ensures that the work package manager feels in control of the discussion and feels that you are listening. It helps the work package manager to feel that his or her ideas are at the heart of the work package.

Sign-off

The completed form should be signed off by the resource owner(s), you and the work package manager. The signed form should then be considered as a contract between you and the work package manager. Sometimes project managers do not bother with the final step of sign-off. After the ongoing discussions leading up to the signing of the work package the signing itself may seem unimportant. Not completing the form by signing it is a mistake. The physical act of signing means that the person concerned is more likely to read through the final presentation of the material. Human nature is such that people will often say they approve a document until they are asked to sign it. Signing the document is a public commitment to the document contents. When faced with adding their approval signature, people normally take extra time to ensure that they have read the material thoroughly and that they agree with the contents.

Once the work package has been signed it should be kept together with any supporting documents in a safe place. All the work packages should be held together and only copies distributed. All work packages should be placed under change control (which is covered in Chapter 3).

WORK BREAKDOWN SUMMARY

You should now be able to produce a final work breakdown structure. The steps taken to reach this stage are:

- Turn the macro plan through 90 degrees, creating a number of potential work packages.
- Interpret and question the results in order to decide the work packages.
- Complete a template for each work package, giving a broad outline and targets for the schedule production.
- Produce an initial schedule using brainstorming techniques.
- Translate the work package and its associated schedule into a set of deliverables.
- From the deliverables, work with experts to produce a schedule.
- Revise all work packages to check all information is coherent.
- Get steering group approval for the plan.

Following the steps outlined should ensure that your project is properly planned and has a completed business case and a completed work breakdown structure. In addition, the people in the project should have a clear understanding of what they personally have to do.

3

Building the detailed project plan

Now that the business case and the associated macro plan and budget are completed you are able to turn your attention to the production of the detailed plan. So far the requirements and tasks generated have all been based on the high-level task groups. Each of these groups now needs to be translated into a detailed task that can be assigned to an individual. For example, you need to translate 'Build the main building' into the myriad of small activities that will need to be carried out in order for the building to be completed.

There are three main activities that you need to complete to produce the detailed plan:

1. Produce the detailed-level requirements.
2. Produce the project schedule.
3. Produce the project plan.

PRODUCE THE DETAILED-LEVEL REQUIREMENTS

The plans that you already have are based on very high-level senior manager ideas. These ideas need to be formally translated into requirements, which in turn need to be translated into a day-to-day plan of work. This plan will change on a day-to-day basis, causing the requirements to change. Subsequently you need to gain and retain control of the requirements of the project if you are to deliver it successfully. There are four main aspects that you need to consider:

1. requirements gathering;
2. requirements in relation to the project life cycle;
3. requirements control systems;
4. change control.

Requirements gathering

Requirements are the requests from the organization to the project that it must fulfil to enable it to satisfy its stakeholders. Unfortunately, because advanced projects have a large volume of requirements, gathering and agreeing them can be difficult. An obvious example might be the building of a new airport. In this illustration there are requirements for lifts, check-in areas, security control, baggage handling, etc. There are far too many requirements for any one individual to understand completely. Instead method becomes important since it is through methodology that control can be retained.

Requirements are generally classified into two categories: high-level requirements (HLRs) and detailed-level requirements (DLRs). Normally a high-level requirement will be broken into many detailed-level requirements. Being able to understand this relationship is essential if the project is to be successful. However, this relationship on its own is not sufficient. You also need to be able to understand the association of the high-level requirement to the work breakdown structure of the project. This ensures that

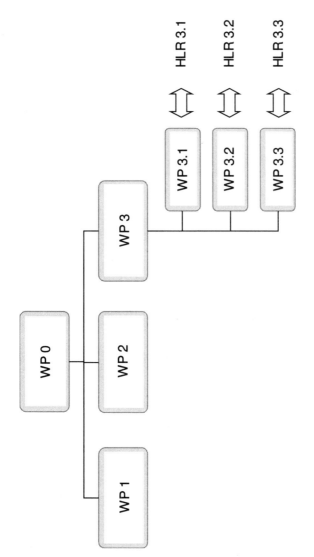

Figure 3.1 High-level requirement derivation from work packages

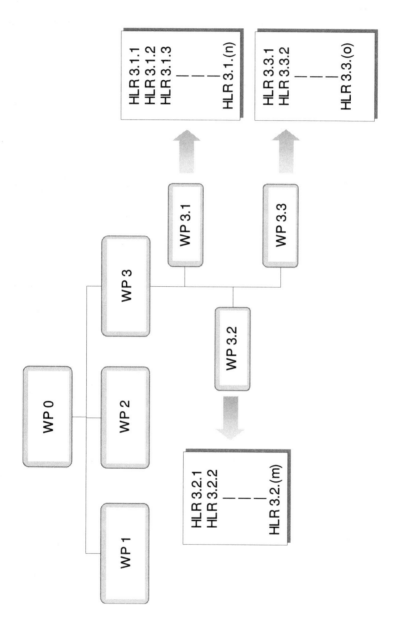

Figure 3.2 High-level requirement number scheme

when a particular task is being reviewed it is easy to understand where the task originated from and who is supposed to be completing it. This is sometimes known as layering the requirements. A simple technique for relating high-level requirements to their associated work package is shown in Figure 3.1.

WP 3 (work package 3) is composed of three separate smaller work packages. For each of these work packages you should define a set of high-level requirements. In their simplest form these high-level requirements might be the tasks covered in the work package description developed during the work described in Chapter 2. However, each high-level requirement should cover only one topic and by the nature of the work undertaken so far it is unlikely that the work package description will do this. Instead it is likely that each work package will need to be revisited and appropriate high-level requirements detailed. The requirements should be related to each other and for clarity they should be contained in a separate document. This is shown in Figure 3.2.

Each high-level requirement has its own unique identifier and that identifier links it to other similar high-level requirements. The unique identifier also links the high-level requirement to the appropriate work package. This scheme can now be extended to include the detailed-level requirements. The detailed-level requirements should be created in response to a specific high-level requirement. This relationship should be reflected in the numbering scheme. This is illustrated in Figure 3.3.

The cross-indexing of high-level requirements and detailed-level requirements ensures that it is easy at all times to identify the trail from any individual requirement back to the work package that is charged with delivering it. This scheme is a simple but effective scheme. There are many schemes available commercially that relate to difficulties that specific industries might have. However, it is always worth while considering this scheme because it is simple and as a result it is easy to manage and understand.

As the requirements gathering starts to gather momentum it is important that you gain and retain control of the incoming

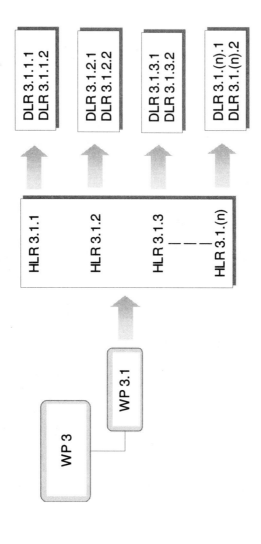

Figure 3.3 HLRs related to DLRs

requirements. With a suitable numbering scheme in place this can be achieved through a simple requirements management process. However, before looking at such a process it is important to understand the difficulties that the project life cycle can bring to requirements capture.

Requirements in relation to the project life cycle

It is not possible to gather all of the requirements at the start of a project. Although your project seems to run to a general life cycle there are actually many sub-life cycles within the overall life cycle. Associated to these sub-life cycles are the high-level requirements and associated with them a series of detailed-level requirements. This is shown diagrammatically in Figure 3.4.

Inexperienced project managers tend to think about their projects in a serial fashion. However, this is rarely the way projects actually happen. Figure 3.4 shows clearly the practical timing of the creation of high-level requirements and their associated detailed-level requirements. The high-level requirements and the detailed-level requirements are created both within an overall project life cycle and within several sub-project life cycles. These sub-projects, which all start at different times, are continually producing high-level requirements and detailed-level requirements. This ongoing process makes it very difficult to define a start and a finish to the requirements capture phase. Coping with this lack of clarity is largely a matter of process. This process doesn't have to be complicated. Instead preference should be given to finding a system that is simple and easy to follow.

Requirements control systems

There are many commercially available requirements management tools. These generally promise to solve all the requirements management issues. However, a simple paper system can prove to be just as effective. Setting up a system is achieved by following a few basic steps:

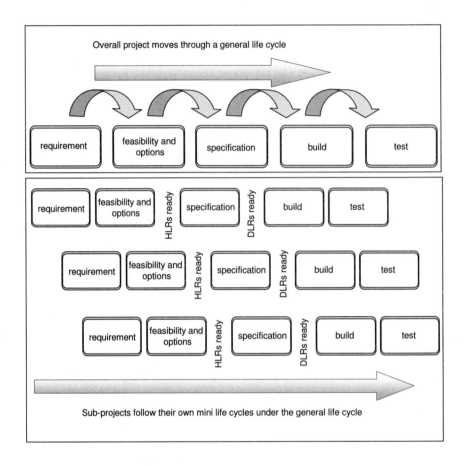

Figure 3.4 HLRs and life cycles

● *Step 1*

Determine a common format that can be used for gathering key information about requirements. A simple word-processor-based template is helpful. It should look something like the form shown in Figure 3.5.

The form should be adjusted to account for the type of tasks that the requirements are being captured for. It is also likely that the form will need to be changed for different project types and perhaps to fit in with the numbering system being used to capture the requirements. Completing the form shown is self-explanatory and should pose you little problem.

Requirement gathering

| **Requirement title:** |
| **Requirement number:** |
| **Related requirements:** |
| **Originator:** |

Description of requirement

Cover here: timescale, scope, resource, quality. Ensure the descriptions are Specific, Measurable, Attainable, Realistic and Time-bound – SMART.

Known constraints

Figure 3.5 Requirements gathering form

- *Step 2*

  Using the previously designed work breakdown structure, identify the work package managers. Explain to them the purpose of the form and ask them to complete the form for their area. Each work package manager should create a list of potential high-level requirements, which should be based on the contents of their work package. This should prove to be a quick exercise, since the work package already contains a list of tasks and deliverables from the work carried out at the macro planning stage. You should explain to the work package managers that this is now the preparation for the detailed requirements gathering phase. As a result they should take the opportunity to revise the form and add in specific high-level requirements associated with their area.

- *Step 3*

All work package managers should now meet with those who have the authority for approving their work packages' high-level requirements. This meeting should cover the process for completing and signing off the high-level requirements. The process will vary from organization to organization with some organizations having whole departments dedicated to understanding and delivering requirements. When there is no in-house department it is useful if the work package manager takes on responsibility for the high-level requirement creation. This is a sensible approach since it is the work package manager who has resources available to undertake the work. It is worth emphasizing to the work package managers that this exercise is not the same as the initial requirements gathering held in support of the production of the macro plan. Instead they are expected to detail out all of the requirements to enable them to deliver the desired project outcome.

- *Step 4*

Once the requirements have been signed off by the relevant customer the next step is the creation of the detailed-level requirements. The easiest way of achieving this is to follow the same process that was used for the generation of the high-level requirements. The only difference is the form that you provide as the standard template for the various work package managers to complete. A revised form is shown in Figure 3.6.

The detailed-level requirement capture should include using the numbering scheme defined for the project. This should be either the scheme provided by the sponsoring organization or one based on the earlier discussion in this chapter.

You should find the form in Figure 3.6 self-explanatory. However, it is worth explaining the two different methods

---

Requirement gathering

DLR reference:
DLR title:
Originator:
HLR reference:

Description of DLR

Cover here: timescale, scope, resource, quality. Ensure the descriptions are Specific, Measurable, Attainable, Realistic and Time-bound – SMART.

Known omissions

Test case

Figure 3.6 DLR gathering form

that can be applied to describe detailed-level requirements. Firstly, detailed-level requirements can be described in a specific measurable form, for example 'There shall be a 1.5-metre fence surrounding the building.' Unfortunately this method does not work for all requirements. When the requirement cannot be made specific then it is best to adopt a scenario approach, for example 'Customers should be delighted with the software and as a result will tell their friends about it.' As the project progresses, the number of requirements that cannot be defined in a measurable way will decrease.

- *Step 5*
  Once the high-level requirements and the detailed-level requirements have been completed they should be included in the project baseline. This will bring them under configuration control. This simply means that prior to any change in day-to-day activity the change must be considered in relation to the requirements.

  If you do decide to adopt a paper system then you should consider setting up a full-time requirements management team. This team should deal with all the requirements and their associated numbering and control. Although requirements management is not a difficult job it does require constant attention, something that you as the project manager will not be able to give it.

Change control

Unlike other projects, advanced projects often have continuous and significant change in their requirements. This large volume of change inevitably results in a substantial number of change requests. This is particularly true at the start of the project. This is when customers generally start to work out what they really want delivered. Controlling this volume effectively is necessary to ensure success in the early project phases. Even as you are in the process of capturing the initial wave of requirements, changes will be happening. It is important that these changes happen in a controlled manner and therefore you should ensure that everyone is using a change control mechanism. A change control mechanism is straightforward to implement. All that you need to do is implement a process that ensures that changes are investigated for their impact prior to the change being made. Again using a simple form helps. A suitable form is shown in Figure 3.7.

Control of the change requests is achieved by the use of the priority and the open and closed date fields. Priority is assigned when the change request is initially raised. For the form shown a

Change control

Priority (0–4):
Change request number:
Change request title:
Sponsor:

Description of proposed change

Cover here: timescale, scope, resource, quality. Ensure the descriptions are Specific, Measurable, Attainable, Realistic and Time-bound – SMART.

Component/tasks affected

Impact on existing plans

Date raised
Date closed

Figure 3.7 Change control form

number between 0 and 4 should be used: 0 is the highest priority and 4 the lowest priority. The level of priority should be suggested by the sponsor (the person raising the change request), but it should be confirmed by someone designated by you. If you have set up a requirements management team then you should delegate the responsibility to them.

Priority setting on its own, however, is not enough to ensure that change requests are being dealt with properly. The length of time a change request has been outstanding also needs to be considered. If the time taken is not considered then those raising change requests will quickly become disillusioned. They will feel that the project simply sets priority levels to avoid dealing with requests. You can easily avoid this situation by setting and adhering to some standard response times, for example:

Priority	Turnaround time
0	2
1	5
2	7
3	10
4	20

So for a priority 0 change request, the project is agreeing that it will deal fully with the proposed change within two days. You need to monitor these times on a regular basis and when the project is consistently failing to meet the set targets you should take remedial action.

PRODUCE THE PROJECT SCHEDULE

As you make progress with the definition of the detailed-level requirements, you will be able to start the production of a project schedule. Project schedules are normally produced as Gantt charts. These charts deliver a wealth of information in a simple graphical format. It is likely that anyone managing an advanced project will already be familiar with them. The chart is constructed in four steps:

1. framework;
2. activity bars;
3. inter-activity dependencies;
4. add risk mitigation.

These are identified in Figure 3.8.

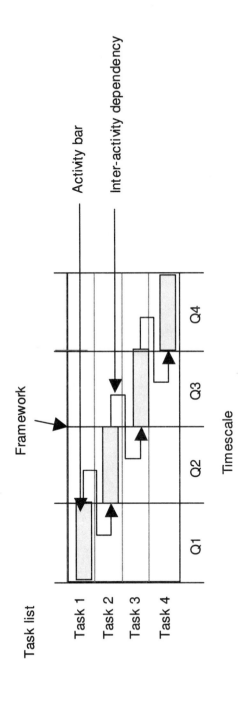

Figure 3.8 Identification of Gantt chart components

Framework

The framework is the mesh of horizontal and vertical lines that form the background of the Gantt chart. The lines create a series of boxes, each of which represents a unit of time. The time line is shown on the horizontal axis at the bottom of the chart. Initially you can set timescale to any arbitrary interval since it will almost certainly change as planning progresses. The timescale shown in Figure 3.8 is set at quarterly intervals since this is a commonly used timescale in advanced projects. If you are using a computer package to generate the chart, adjusting the timescale should be very easy.

The left-hand vertical axis shows the activity list, which is running top to bottom and is labelled from task 1 to task 4. When producing your schedule you should try to use activity descriptions that are meaningful. Ideally all descriptions should be clear, unambiguous and simple. Although in practice this might be difficult to realize fully, it is nevertheless worth while taking some time in the development of the activity names. For example, 'Lay building foundations' or 'Write software test plan' both give a clear indication of the purpose of the activity. If you are producing the Gantt chart using a computer package it is likely that you will be able to annotate the various tasks. These annotations to the activities will enable you to expand on the purpose and meaning of the task.

Activity bars

Activity bars are the backbone of Gantt charts. It is these horizontal bars that show where a task begins and ends. Their visual simplicity hides the amount of information that they present to a knowledgeable reader. Once the framework has been fully populated with activity bars and their inter-dependencies it will hold the majority of the key information needed for analysis and management of the project.

At this stage in the project you should have received from your work package managers a series of tasks along with their time-scale, inter-dependencies and resource needs. You should now populate the framework with only the tasks. If you are using a computer package you will be able to group like tasks together. For example, you might group all of the related work package activities together under one heading. You should quite quickly be able to generate a chart similar (but with many more activities) to the one shown in Figure 3.8 but without the inter-dependencies.

The chart that you have created will now give you a general feel for the likely schedule for the project. However, there is still a substantial amount of work required to enable you to achieve a completed Gantt chart. The next stage in the chart's development is to add the inter-activity dependencies.

Inter-activity dependencies

Adding inter-activity dependencies will link together related tasks. The links are normally shown on a chart as an arrow going between the related activities. There are three inter-dependency types: finish to start, start to start, and finish to finish. The three different types of dependency are shown in Figure 3.9(a), Figure 3.9(b) and Figure 3.9(c).

Finish to start, Figure 3.9(a), is the most common type of inter-activity dependency. It indicates that one task must complete before another can start. In start to start inter-activity dependency, Figure 3.9(b), the tasks involved both must start at the same time; however, this does not imply that the completion of the tasks is synchronized. In finish to finish relationships, Figure 3.9(c), the tasks must complete at the same time. This does not imply that the start of the tasks needs to be synchronized. Often the relationship is not clear and as a result there are two variations that can be used: dependencies with lag time, and partial dependencies. These are shown in Figure 3.10(a) and Figure 3.10(b).

Timescale (weeks)

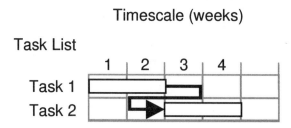

Figure 3.9(a) Finish to start

Timescale (weeks)

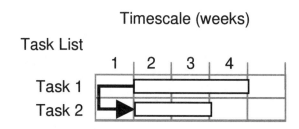

Figure 3.9(b) Start to start

Timescale (weeks)

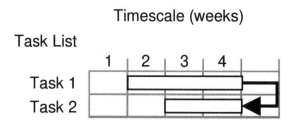

Figure 3.9(c) Finish to finish

You would use an inter-dependency with lag time when a period of time needs to occur between one activity completing and another starting. The example shown in Figure 3.10(a) is when a project needs to obtain planning permission. The request for permission is prepared and agreed with the architect and then the plans are submitted for planning approval. Waiting for the approval takes a number of weeks. During this time it is incorrect to show any project activity since there is none. However, the

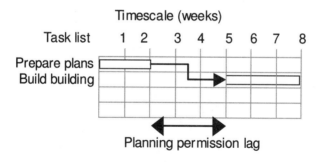

Figure 3.10(a) Finish to start with lag

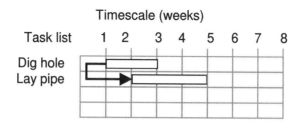

Figure 3.10(b) Start to start with lag

dependency between the tasks remains. Once approval has been given, the building work can start in earnest. Waiting for the planning permission is the lag time, time that must occur between related activities. This type of dependency is called 'finish to start with lag'.

The second variation on inter-dependencies is the partial dependencies. This is used when a task can begin after a certain percentage of its predecessor task (the related task that occurs immediately prior to it) is completed. A simple example of this would be laying a water pipe in a 20-metre-long ditch. The two related activities are digging the ditch and laying the pipe in the ditch. Obviously you do not have to wait for the ditch to be completed before the pipe laying starts. The gang that is laying the pipe will start once a reasonable amount of the ditch has been excavated. This type of activity is called 'start to start with lag' and is shown in Figure 3.10(b).

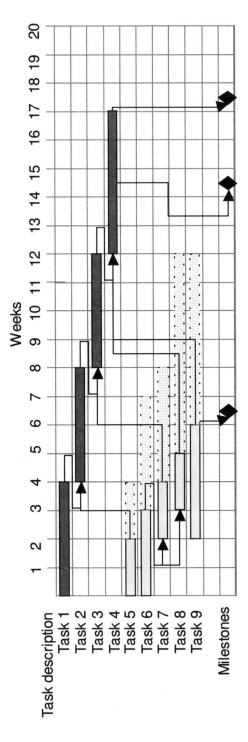

Figure 3.11 Gantt chart with inter-dependencies and float

You should now have a Gantt chart that has the various project tasks and their inter-dependencies shown. It will be similar to but larger than the chart shown in Figure 3.11.

The chart shows that task 4 is the last task to finish, finishing in week 17. The series of activities leading up to week 17 are task 1 followed by task 2 and then by task 3. These four tasks are known as the critical path of the project. The critical path of the project is a very important feature of the chart and is one that you should identify for your project. The critical path shows tasks that occur serially and immediately after one another from the start of the project until its end. All of the tasks must finish and start on time (or earlier) for the entire project to finish to its published schedule. The activities that form the critical path are known as critical tasks. Project managers normally highlight the critical path by using a different colour or shade of grey for the activities that lie on it.

Tasks that are not on the critical path have float attached to them. Technically, float is the difference between the time available for completing a task and the time required to complete the task. If a task has no float then it is on the critical path of the project. A subset of float is known as free float. This is the maximum amount of time by which a task can be delayed beyond its start date without delaying any successor task beyond its start date. Free float will only appear on tasks that have a successor that is not on the critical path.

Float is shown attached to each of the non-critical tasks shown in Figure 3.11. It is the additional bar that is visible beyond the end of the activity bar. For example, task 6 can slip by up to four weeks without affecting the end date of the project. If it slips by a further one week then it would make the project one week late. This would happen because it would make task 7 one week late, which in turn would make task 3 one week late. The greatest amount of float is attached to task 8 and is seven weeks in length. This means that it can slip by up to seven weeks without having any effect on the end date of the project

This chart is now more or less complete and if it depicted your project it would be possible to use it for managing your project.

However, there are three black diamonds that have not been mentioned so far, which have been included to improve the chart's usefulness. The diamonds are used to depict project milestones, which are key points in the project's life when a major event will have been completed. For example, the event might be the completion of the requirements and functional specification. Often companies will use a formal methodology that dictates what milestone events contain. You should assess this and set some project milestones as needed.

In addition to the formal milestones it is worth while considering the addition of some interim milestones. These can be used to add additional focus for the project team to enable them to view progress as the project goes forward. The completion of these milestones is especially important on advanced projects where the distance between the formal milestones can be many months.

Add risk mitigation

All projects have a degree of uncertainty (or risk) associated with them. This can happen for various reasons, for example because the company has not undertaken similar work before. Whatever the reason for the uncertainty it is sensible to prepare for activities not delivering according to plan. A common mistake of inexperienced project managers is to believe that careful initial planning will enable them to eliminate the risk in the project. Therefore once they have completed the initial plan they see little point in expending more energy on introducing risk mitigation. However, unseen events will always occur, for example a flu epidemic may occur. So you should allow time in your plan for things to go wrong.

There are two standard methods for showing additional time in a project. The first method has already been discussed, float. The second method is called the 'addition of contingency'. You should be careful to avoid confusing the two methods. They are very different in nature. Both can be successfully used to provide time that can compensate for things going wrong. The difference between the two is their relationship to the end date of the project. If contingency is used then the project will have slipped past its earliest possible end date. This is different to float, which is time that is available but if used won't affect the end date of the project.

Obviously both are useful but it would be unwise for you to rely on float to save your project when things go wrong. You should include contingency for each task in your project where there is a significant risk of the task not staying on its original schedule. You should add it on a task-by-task basis, allowing you to add more contingency on higher-risk tasks than on lower-risk tasks.

One difficulty that you will face when adding contingency to your project is reluctance from the project steering group. They will be keen that the project finishes as quickly as possible and as a result they will not be keen to add time that might not be needed. Often members of the steering group suggest that contingency is added in a block at the end of the project rather than on a task-by-task basis. If possible you should resist this suggestion. You should remind them that only certain tasks need contingency and that adding it at the end will seem like a licence to slip on all tasks. If contingency is added to the plan in Figure 3.11 then it will be redrawn as shown in Figure 3.12.

One week of contingency has been added to task 4 and one week to task 5. Since task 4 is on the critical path this has resulted in a one-week slip to the end of the project. However, the addition of the contingency to task 5 has had no overall effect except reducing the duration of the float for the task.

You should now have a complete project schedule. This accompanied by the detailed-level requirements should be presented to the steering group at the next scheduled meeting. At the meeting you should inform the group that you intend that this plan form the baseline of the project. If the plan differs significantly from the macro plan already presented as part of the business case you will need to discuss the implications with the steering group members.

If the steering group approves your proposed baseline plan then you will have achieved a significant milestone in the project. This plan agreed at this milestone will be the plan against which

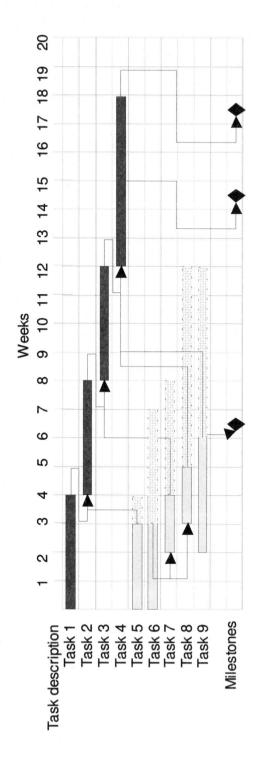

Figure 3.12 Gantt chart with contingency

you are measured. Although plans can and do change, this baseline will always remain as a footprint in time against which the organization will measure success. It will help the organization understand whether it is achieving what it wanted to achieve.

PRODUCE THE PROJECT PLAN

Now that most major decisions have been made and the steering group have approved the schedule it is helpful if everything is recorded in one place. This is usually achieved by producing a project plan. Project plans vary from project to project, because of the diverse nature of the topics they have to cover. This is emphasized more with advanced projects since the projects tend to undertake work that may be new to the organization. However, despite the diversity of content all project plans for advanced projects do have certain common characteristics. Topics that must be covered in the plan are:

● overview of the project;
● control structure and driving mechanisms;
● project organization and structure;
● expected project life cycle;
● key deliverables;
● costs or resource usage.

● *Overview of the project*
The overview of the project can probably be taken directly from the introduction to the business case. This will provide a discussion of the purpose and the objective of the project. You will need to add to this details that will have been developed since the business case was written. In particular you should add details of the requirements and key project milestones.
● *Control structure and driving mechanisms*
The control structure and driving mechanisms are discussed more fully in Chapter 6. However, at the simplest level you

can include details of the key principals and their roles and responsibilities. These were developed during the initiation phase of the project under the theme of defining early roles and responsibilities.

- *Project organization and structure*
  The project organization and structure should be reasonably well defined by now. The structure that is required, however, is not an organization chart that covers everyone in the project. Instead it is a chart showing the key principals and the key groups and meetings that are in place, for example the project steering group.
- *Expected project life cycle*
  Depending on the organization you may need to define a life cycle for the project. Many organizations will have their own life cycle and where this is available you should use it. However, in some cases you will need to adjust the life cycle to reflect the unique nature of your project. Throughout this book there are examples of life cycles that could be used.
- *Key deliverables*
  You will have agreed by now with the steering group a number of deliverables that they want to see resulting from the work of the project. These should be listed along with appropriate success criteria. Wherever possible you should include a quality statement against each deliverable.
- *Costs or resource usage*
  Costs can be covered by using the material developed in support of the business case. They should cover both the capital costs and the revenue costs. In some cases it will be inappropriate to add the costs to the plan, especially when the plan is to be made public. When this happens you should simply drop this section from the plan.

Often there is discussion about whether the project plan should contain all of these sections and the details contained within them. Many people suggest that there should be separate plans for each topic and that there is significant overlap with other documents already in existence. They would like the project plan simply to refer them to the relevant plan or document. The difficulty with this approach is that many readers will never reach the other plans. Instead they will peruse the project plan and finding little of interest will not become more knowledgeable about the project. Therefore you should produce one plan that covers all of these topics.

When you produce the plan you need to be careful to ensure that you maintain a good balance between repeating information in other plans and putting sufficient information to enable the reader to understand what is proposed. A reasonable way to approach this is to set aside one page per topic (or 400 words). This would mean six pages to cover the topics above. As with previous sizing, this makes authors careful with their words – ideal when communicating with senior managers. Once completed the plan should be agreed by the project steering group and published for access by all project team members.

4

Building the project team

To achieve a successful project you need a successful project team. Without a strong team the expectations of the organization will not be met because the project will fail to deliver. You need to remember that the team is not only the people working directly on the project. Your team is all of the people involved, either directly or indirectly. All of these people are needed to ensure success or failure in the eyes of the sponsoring organization. It is your role to bring this team together and enable them to deliver the organization's demands. You cannot deliver success by yourself; you need a team to help you.

To achieve this you need to consider four areas with respect to team building and motivation:

1. Define the project team.
2. Motivate the project team.
3. Listen to the project team.
4. Gain the respect of the project team.

DEFINE THE PROJECT TEAM

Mapping out who is involved in the project is the first step in building your project team. The most obvious place to start the definition of the project team is to use the existing who's who spreadsheet that was developed during the initiation phase of the project (see Table 1.2). Potentially this could enable you to determine at least an initial group of people who need to be included as part of the project team. However, the who's who spreadsheet does not cover all of the people in the project and it may not have been kept up to date as new people joined the project. It is also probable that the spreadsheet doesn't show how the various people listed relate to one another in terms of work on the project.

Unless you have spent effort on keeping the project's who's who directory up to date it is probably more productive to start with the work breakdown structure when determining the project team. This is a simple but effective way of identifying a large number of team members quickly. It also has the benefit of linking together team members who are undertaking similar or related activities. This analysis should allow you to produce a team organization chart. The chart should be similar in style to the chart shown in Figure 4.1.

This chart shows the names and some key information about each person. Additionally it shows the project reporting relationship of one person to another. However, the chart also clearly shows one of the difficulties that advanced projects pose when you are building an organization chart. Advanced projects have a large number of people working on them and this makes it difficult to display the information in a manner that allows it to be easily accessed. This can be overcome by drawing a separate chart for each work package and if necessary a separate chart for any sub-work packages.

When all the charts have been completed you should have a suite of papers that collectively set out the organizational chart for the project. Before considering publishing this chart you need to address those people who may not have been included in the

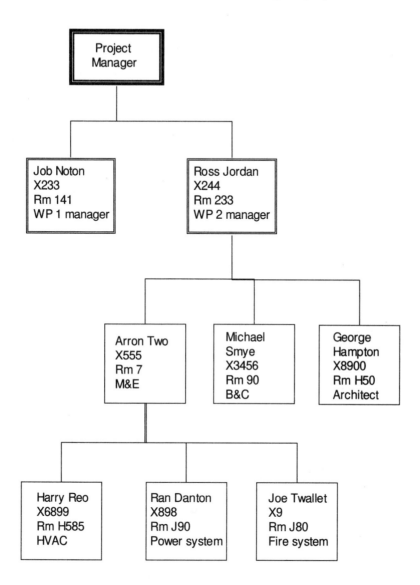

Figure 4.1 Project organization chart

work breakdown structure. You need to seek out those people who are on the periphery of the project and add them to the chart.

Project managers sometimes find it difficult to decide who they should include in the chart and who should remain absent. They spend a disproportionate amount of time worrying about whether someone will be offended about being left off the chart. Often they avoid the question by including everyone they can think of. This is unnecessary and clogs up the chart, making it harder for team members to find those people they are searching for. You do not need to do this.

To determine who should be included in the chart you should analyse the meetings that are held in support of the project and include the people who are involved in them on the chart. This works effectively since the project meetings that are interwoven through a project are normally generated by interest in the project. Many of these meetings are not driven by the needs of the project but by the desire of those outside the project to influence the day-to-day activity. Therefore gathering a list of these meetings, their purpose and membership can prove to be an effective method of identifying team members. The list generated is likely to include senior managers, the project sponsor and people external to the organization, for example customers. Once all of the potential project team members have been identified your initial organizational chart should be updated and published.

Rather than presenting this information in a paper format it is more effective to consider using an electronic publishing method. Perhaps the simplest method is to incorporate the material into a Web page that all of the people in the project have access to. Using a Web-based approach can prove effective since it is easier to keep it up to date and avoids the expense of republishing the chart suite every time there is a change in team personnel.

When the chart is published you should take time to ensure that those involved in the project know that a new chart is available. As the project progresses there will be smaller changes as the team make-up changes. Therefore it is good practice to establish a method of informing team members of changes at the start of the project. The simplest way of achieving this is simply to send an e-mail to the people on the chart.

MOTIVATE THE PROJECT TEAM

Although it is important to ensure that your project team has the right set of skills to enable it to deliver the project on time, it is often not this that lets it down. Instead it is a lack of motivation to use the skills that it has that is the issue. Generally it is better to have someone who is highly motivated with average skills than someone who has brilliant skills but doesn't really care. Although there are always exceptions to this rule, you as project manager need to think in broad terms about the people in the project. Most of them will conform to this general categorization method. Highly motivated is when they will be the most effective. There are two ways that work well when motivating teams and their members: 1) motivating the team by incentives; 2) motivating the team by delegation.

Motivating the team by incentives

This is perhaps the most obvious way to motivate your project team and in some respects it is still one of the best ways of motivating the team. Incentives can take many forms, for example movie tickets or cash, and they can be given in public or in private. They can also be very immediate in their impact since they can be given immediately something good has happened.

Incentive giving can be driven by a formal scheme or by an ad hoc scheme. Normally a formal scheme will set out objectives that need to be met in order to receive a specific reward. These incentive schemes are sometimes termed 'performance management' or 'bonus schemes'. Many organizations however only operate these schemes for their more senior managers and as a result a separate scheme is required within a project.

Often the best schemes achieve the motivation of team members by spontaneous thanks for completing a task successfully. This is the ad hoc-based approach. Some project managers are wary of this approach because they fear alienating members of the team who do not receive rewards. But you should not let this fear stop you from adopting an ad hoc approach. Providing there is some discussion and the reward is not substantial then any difficulties arising are likely to be small.

Deciding on the incentives to be given to the project team can prove to be a fun activity. It is always enjoyable to think about ways of making others happy and excited. One of the most effective types of reward is the use of project merchandise. This helps to create a project identity and reminds receivers that they got the reward for working on a specific project. It also helps to build team spirit. It makes the team member feel part of a group, the group that's delivering the project.

Developing a project merchandise list can be turned into a team-building exercise. This is achieved by using a four-step approach:

- *Step 1*
  Gather together the work package managers and any other key project team members. Explain to them that the purpose of the meeting is to have some fun but the result will help the project deliver more successfully. You should describe to the participants the idea of the ad hoc incentive scheme and tell them that you want them to come up with a list of ad hoc rewards.
- *Step 2*
  Run a brainstorm session using the technique described previously. Encourage those present to draw up a list of ideas for project merchandise. As before, give everyone their own pad of paper. Let them write down ideas for up to 10 minutes before pinning the lists up on the wall. Give permission to those present to let their imagination run wild. Tell them that you will be disappointed if there is not the odd helicopter and private jet alongside the more down-to-earth pens and key-rings.
- *Step 3*
  After the meeting, develop the list of ideas and subsequently produce a first-draft merchandise list. Remove from this list items that are clearly unrealistic, for example the helicopter.

Table 4.1 Merchandise cost table

Item	Unit cost	Number of units	Total cost
Plastic pens	£0.10	3	£0.30
Metal pens	£1.00	5	£5.00
Business card holder	£3.00	10	£30.00
T-shirt	£10.00	15	£150.00
Jacket	£40.00	12	£480.00
Total			£665.30

- *Step 4*
  Create a final list with pricing against each item. A typical list might be similar to the one shown in Table 4.1.

Once the list has been completed and the price of each item worked out, a project incentive scheme budget needs to be developed. The budget should simply set out an estimate of the quantity of each item required and the total overall cost. Once you have the budget prepared you should seek to get it approved. Getting approval for it however can often prove to be difficult. Often organizations don't understand the benefit of spending funds on project merchandise. People within the organization view spending on merchandise as frivolous and a waste of precious funds. This view must be expected and you should have robust arguments ready. There are two obvious benefits.

The first benefit is a sense of belonging. People like to belong to something. They particularly like this when there are other people involved. For project team members it is very motivating to be sitting in a canteen (or similar) and see someone they don't know wearing a project T-shirt (or using a project pen). It confirms to them that people value the work they are involved in and that others want to be part of it.

The second benefit is publicity for the project. Publicity is like oxygen to an advanced project: it needs it to survive. This may seem melodramatic but in most cases it stands up to analysis.

Advanced projects normally involve undertaking work that affects people's lives. For example, imagine building a new road without any discussion with the residents whose life will be affected. Or imagine designing a new air traffic control system without involving the air traffic controllers. The people affected need to be identified and informed. Unfortunately, it will not be possible to identify easily all those affected and so publicity is required. The publicity helps to reduce the risk that people affected by the project's outcome don't know of the project. Publicity helps to ensure that as many people as possible are reached.

If these arguments fail, you might consider trying to put through a smaller amount for the project budget. Try to build the budget up as the project progresses. This approach can work well since the amounts involved will often be dwarfed by the main project budget. This makes those in charge of the budget less likely to question the budget line item.

Motivating the team by delegation

Despite the obvious motivational aspects of incentives they are not sufficient to ensure that the project team is inspired. Building a team needs to go beyond mugs and pens to be inspirational. It needs you to empower people so that they feel they are adding value and not simply doing what they are told. To achieve this you must put in place a clearly defined delegation structure.

Delegation can be defined as the ability to let go without losing control. If achieved successfully, team members will feel valued and trusted. However, delegating authority and responsibility can prove to be a difficult task if you are an inexperienced project manager. To be successful, delegation requires you to have faith and belief in your project team. If you want to be successful it is a skill that you need to learn. It is not possible for you to know what all of the people in the project are doing. You must delegate authority to act or you will drown in a sea of tasks over which you will quickly lose control and perspective.

It is worth remembering that you have already started the delegation process with the creation of the work packages and so you should already have some experience of what to expect from your team. If the experience is good so far then go quickly and if not then go slowly with delegation.

The work packages have boundaries that outline what a work package manager can and cannot do. This initial delegation needs to be continued and it should be cascaded throughout the project. You should ask the work package managers to follow your lead and split their authority and control into manageable groups of work. The work package managers should then be encouraged to delegate authority for these groups of work to their team members. To encourage consistency in approach across the project it is useful for all the work package managers to use a standard in-house form. If the organization does not have such a form then one similar to the one in Figure 4.2 should be created and used.

Work Package Name
Description
Add a brief description of the activities that will be undertaken. This should specify the purpose of the work and the method by which that purpose will be met.
Resources
Add a list of the resources that will be available to the team member as an aid to achieving the expected result.
Expected outcome
List the deliverables: scope, timescale, quality including test measurement.
Risks
Add here a list of the risks. These should be agreed at the meeting.
Approvals
Add here the signatures of the work package manager and the team member along with the date the agreement was made. Leave a copy of the signed form with the team member.

Figure 4.2 Team member task agreement form

The form itself does not guarantee successful delegation of a task or a group of tasks. This is achieved through the skill of the work package manager in the delegation process. It is likely that all of the work package managers will believe that they are expert at delegating tasks. However, it is unlikely that they will all be at the same standard and so it is helpful to provide a short refresher course for them. Holding a short course, perhaps one hour in duration, will ensure that the work package managers have the opportunity to remind one another of best practice. The course will also ensure that a consistent approach will be used across the project.

Your organization may already have an in-house delegation teaching course that you could consider using. However, you should remember that, although these are normally well written and in some cases effective, they are probably not useful for the audience intended by you. These courses tend to be one or two days in duration and they are often aimed at junior people in the organization. The objective of your course is to remind the participants about good delegation practices, not to teach them it. If a short course exists that will achieve this then you should consider it. However, often it will be simpler and quicker for you to set up a course yourself.

The course should take the form of a discussion meeting and from the outset you should be careful to explain that the purpose of the course is to gain from one another's experience about delegation. You should be vocal in expressing that the purpose is not to teach delegation methods but instead to gain knowledge from managers who are already experienced in delegation. At the meeting you should make a short presentation on delegation and how to achieve it effectively. The presentation should be followed by a discussion amongst the work package managers. There are four key thoughts that you should ensure are discussed by the meeting participants:

- *Thought one*
  The first action the work package manager should take is to set up a meeting to delegate authority for a task formally. At

the meeting the work package manager should produce the delegation form and should discuss it in detail with the team member. Initially the discussion should centre on the content and purpose of the form rather than the content of the task to be delegated. Work package managers should remember that the form is probably a new concept to many of the team members and as such it is worth while spending time reviewing its contents. Ideally prior to the meeting the work package manager should tell the team member that he or she wants to hold a delegation meeting and should give the team member some idea of what he or she wants to discuss. This gives the team member time to think about the task and about the delegation process prior to the meeting. Once the work package manager is confident the team member understands the form, the manager should discuss the task to be delegated.

- *Thought two*
Before the meeting the work package manager should set aside time to consider the ability of the team member to whom the task or task group is being delegated. Although some of the skills will be task-specific many of them will be part of a general skill set. When considering the skills required, the work package manager should remember that the objective is to identify where the team member's skills are weak and therefore where it is likely that support will be needed. By doing this the work package manager will be reducing the risk in the work package.

- *Thought three*
Once the form is complete the work package manager and the team member should set it aside for a few days before meeting again to review the completed form. Both the team member and the work package manager should be clear at this second meeting about their expectations surrounding the task and its likely outcome. It is important that the team member leaves the meeting feeling supported in his or her work. The work package manager should avoid the team member feeling criticized.

- *Thought four*

   Many work package managers will view filling out any form
   with suspicion. They often don't understand the benefits.
   They believe that it is the start of a paperwork mountain that
   they will have to climb and that that mountain will slow
   everything down. It is important that you deal effectively
   with this issue. The reasons for using a form are:
   - Forms provide a simple reminder to the experienced work
     package manager and a useful tool to the inexperienced
     work package manager. They help to ensure that all of the
     key points are discussed with the team member.
   - Forms provide a record that can be returned to periodic-
     ally to ensure that tasks delegated are being completed
     effectively.
   - Forms ensure that a consistent approach is used for delega-
     tion of tasks within the project. This provides two benefits.
     Firstly, a team member's perception is enhanced because
     he or she sees a consistent and professional approach. This
     is particularly important with more junior team members.
     Secondly, it reduces the learning curve should there be a
     change in work package manager or team member since
     they will already be familiar with the format of the form.

At the end of the meeting the work package manager and the
team member should have agreed the delegated tasks and the
parameters accompanying those tasks. They should also have
agreed any support they need to ensure that they can undertake
their work successfully.

Where possible the forms should be stored in a central computer system that allows easy access from any computer. This
enables people working on other tasks to view the delegation
sheet and understand more clearly who is doing what. This can
be particularly powerful when used in conjunction with the
project organization chart.

LISTEN TO THE PROJECT TEAM

After establishing the formal structures and delegating authority to act to the project teams, you need to move your focus on to listening to the project team. Listening to the team after establishing the formal structures is very important. It is only through listening to the team that you will be able to discover where the established structure is failing.

Project managers generally have pushy personalities and they are forceful when making a point during discussion. These characteristics are helpful when driving a project forward. However, these same characteristics can make it very difficult when trying to get a team to tell you where things are going wrong. Project managers have a tendency to listen to the first few sentences and then jump in with solutions.

If you want to run advanced-level projects well you need to be aware of your personality and its characteristics. You need to learn to control the characteristics and use them selectively. There are two basic techniques, push and pull.

The push technique is the technique that most people, especially project managers, feel comfortable with. This technique involves forming an opinion and then arguing for it. This is an adversarial technique where the emphasis is on pushing a developed opinion until convinced otherwise by argument. Most meetings that project managers and the project team members attend will use this method of communication.

The pull technique is the opposite of the push technique. Rather than giving an opinion and then trying to convince others it is correct, the pull technique relies on seeking the opinion of others. The pull technique is sometimes wrongly thought of as simply asking questions. This is too simplistic an interpretation. Instead the person using the technique should form an opinion and then use skilful questioning to encourage others to form the same opinion. The pull technique however generally takes longer to achieve a decision.

Neither technique is sufficient on its own. A skilful project manager needs to use both techniques, depending on the situation. For most project managers this means redeveloping their listening skills. They need to relearn skills that were at some stage excellent.

Listening skills fall into two general categories, passive and active listening. Passive listening is when the person listening simply sits trying to take in the information being given. Active listening is when the person listening takes notes and often asks questions to ensure that he or she fully understands what is being said. Active listening is what advanced project managers should learn to excel at.

To listen actively to a team member you need to check continually that you have correctly interpreted what you are being told. This is easily achieved by simply summarizing back to the speaker what you have heard. However, you should take care not to break up the speaker's speech continually!

Active listening when undertaken effectively ensures that speakers know they are being understood. It makes team members feel valued and makes them feel it is worth making a contribution.

GAIN THE RESPECT OF THE PROJECT TEAM

Despite all of your efforts to motivate the team and to make their work life enjoyable it can still be hard to gain their respect. You have a tough job. You have to lead the team, listen and respond to the team and take the criticism of the team. Whilst this is going on you need to remain positive and act as a project leader should.

Gaining your team's respect is a very hard job. It can only be achieved through being consistent and delivering according to any promises that have been made. You need to follow through continually on what you have promised. No matter how fed up with things you are you need to be positive and lead from the front.

Although it is difficult, you need to re-establish continually all of the methods for building a team described in this chapter. There need to be a continual renewal and a continuing injection of fresh ideas. It is only through this re-establishment of authority and team player attitude that you will be able to be sure that a successful team is being developed.

5

How to run the project on a day-to-day basis

Running the project on a day-to-day basis is the job most project managers enjoy the most. Most do not like spending their time working through the paperwork necessary to get the project up and running. Nor do most project managers enjoy all the ongoing administration necessary to keep the project running. Instead typical project managers like this phase of the project where lots of work is progressing and they get to talk with those actually producing deliverables.

Although this can be one of the most hectic phases for the project manager it can also be one of the most rewarding. To ensure that everything goes as smoothly as possible there are a number of areas you need to work through:

- What is the type of project that you are going to run?
- What is the strategy for the execution of your project?
- How will you implement the execution strategy?
- How can you ensure that quality remains on the agenda?
- Have you ensured that those involved clearly understand their role?

WHAT IS THE TYPE OF PROJECT THAT YOU ARE GOING TO RUN?

Advanced projects fall into several categories: mixed projects, in-house projects and outsourced projects. Each of these has its own characteristics and benefits. Often you will find that one type of project dominates the way that a particular organization does business. For example, some organizations only believe in using internal staff to work on new software releases. They believe the work is too sensitive to be run by external organizations. To achieve success with your project you need to understand the different project types and work out which dominates within your organization's culture. You then need to adjust your method of working to fit with that culture.

Mixed projects

Advanced projects often require organizations to work in areas that are new and unknown to them. A good example is an organization building a new headquarters. Although the organization may have a facilities management capability, it is unlikely to have experience of building buildings. To overcome this difficulty the organization would probably hire external help, for example in this illustration it might hire architects. Mixed projects work primarily because they allow effective risk management. They allow organizations to use external resources to supply the skills that they do not have in-house.

It is not only external resources that organizations need to contract to enable them to complete advanced projects. Frequently organizations need to hire a new project manager to run the advanced project they want to complete. Project managers of advanced projects rarely remain with one organization for their whole career. This is because organizations do not commonly undertake several advanced projects in a row. Instead advanced projects tend to happen infrequently in response to strategic business model changes. As a result, project managers tackling these projects tend to move to other organizations at the end of the project.

If the organization has an advanced project manager in place for the project then it normally falls to him or her to decide what type of project should be undertaken. The decision is always likely to remain a matter of judgement. However, there are some influences that should be accounted for and some factors that should be considered before a judgement call is made. The influences to consider are relatively simple to understand. They are simply the opinions of the key stakeholders of the project. If substantial external resource is to be used then the key stakeholders need to agree that this is the right way forward. It is a judgement that needs to be made in alliance with the stakeholders of the organization. The factors to consider are slightly more complex. You should consider:

- the macro plan;
- the skills profile of the team;
- the volume of available resources.

The macro plan is a good place for you to start considering the benefits of a mixed project. The plan sets out all the known work tasks and associated schedules. This provides you with an easy reference for the main tasks that the project might need to undertake. You simply need to assess each of the activities in order to determine whether these activities are in sympathy with the organization's core business. If they are not similar then you would need to create a new team to be able to complete them in-house. Unless there is good reason for this it is probably more sensible to use an outsource solution.

The macro plan will also provide a good source of information to allow you to assess the skills profile required for the project team. You need to examine this skills profile to determine the skills needed to complete the project. You need to exercise caution when doing this work. Although the team may seem at first glance to have the required skill set, they may be inexperienced.

Often one of the trickier jobs for you is to explain to your team that they are not sufficiently experienced and that external people will need to be brought in. This is especially difficult with advanced projects since by and large it is these projects that the people within an organization want to work on. After all, these are the projects that are leading the future of the organization.

The macro plan is also the source that allows you to determine the volume of staff required for the project. Normally advanced projects need substantially more people than the sponsoring organization has. This volume is driven by simply having enough people to run the existing organization's business plus enough people to complete the advanced project. If the organization needs to double in size to make the project a reality then it is likely that outsourcing will be needed. There is little point in doubling the size of the organization for one project. The organization would need to be able to find jobs for all of the new people. If it could not find employment for the new people then it might have to make them redundant – a cost it will want to avoid.

Once all of these factors have been considered with the stake-holders you should be in a good position to decide whether this project type is suitable. However before finally deciding you should consider the other types of project: in-house and out-sourced.

In-house

This project type is normally undertaken when the work concerned is central to the business of the organization. An example might be the production of a new software product. In this example it is likely that the organization will have sufficient developers in-house. These developers may be ideal to build a new product.

One of the most persuasive aspects of an in-house project is the level of control available to the organization. Since there are no contract penalties involved, the organization is free to change its mind on an ongoing basis. This is attractive to organizations, particularly when they remain unsure of the final outcome of an advanced project.

Many organizations view an in-house resourced project as the best type of project. Often they do not fully understand the risks. Advanced projects that are undertaken in-house face two major risk areas. Firstly, the high levels of control generally result in the organization changing its mind frequently. This constant change results in the organization and you facing costs that may be substantially increased. Secondly, with this type of project there is a significant risk of process protection.

An advanced project is very likely to require an organization to work in a way that is new. Existing processes need to be reinvented and new ones added. Unfortunately, people in an in-house project often don't share this view. The in-house project staff do not understand the need to change their existing methods of working. In many cases this goes further and they believe that they are being criticized when change is suggested. They don't understand that larger, more difficult projects generally need to do things differently.

Advanced project managers need to exercise a significant degree of patience with an in-house project. They must be sensitive to the staff and they need to take time to build consensus on the need for new processes. For processes, a simple way to achieve this consensus is to set up a project quality steering group. The purpose of a project quality steering group is to manage the new processes being used within the project. The group also manages the relationship between the project and the sponsoring organization. This helps to ensure that best practice is picked up by the organization. Some suggested terms of reference might be:

- The quality steering group maintains an awareness of the process initiatives within the organization.
- The quality steering group will act as the project function to ensure the success of all process-related initiatives.
- The quality steering group will own all process-associated activities.

- The members of the quality steering group will act as the change catalysts within the project.
- Members of the quality steering group will evangelize process improvements. They will do this by generating motivation and enthusiasm for process improvement within the project.
- The quality steering group members are: [add here the names of the members of the steering group].

Outsourced

The third project type is the outsourced project. This could be more accurately described as a fully outsourced project. With this project type all of the work is given to an external company for completion and delivery. This company then assumes the risk and also reaps a substantial reward if it delivers successfully. A large number of government projects are undertaken as fully outsourced projects. This happens because of the diversity of the work that a government is required to undertake. It is unrealistic to expect a government to employ everyone needed for every type of advanced project.

Outsourced projects carry substantial financial risk for the sponsoring organization. All of the detail of the project work is controlled and run by others outside of the organization. These people have their own organizations to satisfy as well as the commissioning organization. Sometimes this results in a conflict of interest. A very simple example might be when an outsourced supplier may need to choose whether to paint a building with paint that will last 10 years or 2 years. Both might be acceptable within the contract framework. However, the maintenance cost could obviously be reduced by using the 10-year paint. If the people making the decision worked for the commissioning organization they would probably pick the 10-year paint. However if they worked for the supplying organization they might pick the 2-year paint. It is likely that the 2-year paint is cheaper and that their organization will benefit from a higher maintenance cost (that is, their company will be painting the building every 2 years instead of every 10 years). In outsourced projects it is therefore extremely important that you are well versed in the contract structure. Knowing the structure and the likely pitfalls is likely to save the sponsoring organization substantial funds.

The key to success for this type of project is in understanding how to gain control effectively over the actions of the outsourced company. This is achieved by introducing the concept of various levels of control. Introducing levels will help you more effectively manage the risks of the project. The levels that should be used are: high-risk items, medium-risk items and low-risk items. All of the activities within the project should be split into one of these three groups.

The low-risk items in general can be handed over to the out-source company. Control can probably be freely given. You can be confident that the items concerned will not substantially affect the project outcome. It is likely that these items will form over 50 per cent of the project activities. This leaves you free to concentrate on the medium- and high-risk items.

Medium- and high-risk items require a reasonable level of control. The simplest way of exercising control is by requiring the supplier to gain acceptance for all plans. For project managers not used to running outsourced contracts this may seem a drastic suggestion. Inexperienced project managers often worry that the outsourced company will be upset and the relationship difficult. However, it is an accepted method of working, and generally outsourced companies will be happy to work in this way. The outsource company will put restrictions on the turnaround time for approval of the plans submitted. Often this turnaround time is set at 10 days. The approval method should be set out in the contract.

The advanced project scenario

It is unlikely that all of an advanced project will be outsourced or that all of the project will be run in-house. Mixed projects are almost always the dominant project type. This means that a project manager has to be skilled at handling both internal and external resources.

Handling external resources

The key to working with external organizations is to pick one that will work in sympathy with your organization. To do this efficiently and effectively some form of rating scheme or system is desirable. Rating systems are often already in place within organizations, many of which have some form of approved vendors list. This list is the starting point for a rating system. Approved vendors lists are set up by large organizations to enable them to deal consistently with suppliers. To get on to an approved vendors list, suppliers normally have to undergo some form of assessment. The assessment will often include a questionnaire and in some cases will include an on-site audit. The objective from the buying organization's viewpoint is to ensure consistency across all suppliers used. The assessment is frequently known as 'due diligence'.

An approved vendors list is not however a rating system. Some organizations are very diligent in keeping their vendors lists up to date. Unfortunately most are not. The rigour that is applied in assessing whether a company should be allowed on to the list is often not applied in assessing whether it should remain on the list.

Project managers for advanced projects must first understand the status of any list. If the list includes some form of continuous upgrade and rating they should consider using it without doing any further work. If the list doesn't include any form of upgrade then some form of work will need to be undertaken to revamp the list to an acceptable level of quality. Turning an existing approved vendors list into an approved supplier rating system is reasonably simple.

The first activity is to decide the criteria with which to assess the proposed vendors. Some companies will already have criteria that they particularly care about. However, these are unlikely to be centred on the needs of the advanced project. Suitable criteria for a project have to centre on the four underlying principles for

Table 5.1 Supplier assessment criteria

Area	Criteria ID	Criteria description
Scope	1	Well versed in cladding systems
Scope	2	Able to build in remote locations
Quality	3	Has strong quality plan
Quality	4	Can provide excellent testimonials
Timescale	5	Has proven track record of delivering on time
Timescale	6	Has proven track record of accurate estimation
Resource	7	Always comes in on budget
Resource	8	Is good value in cost terms

advanced project management: scope, quality, timescale and resource. For each of these you should define criteria you feel match the project's needs. For example, a building project might have the criteria shown in Table 5.1.

These criteria can then be scored and the results cross-matched against suppliers. The marking should be carried out by people within the organization and should be arranged by the project manager. A sample results table is shown in Table 5.2.

The table shows a score for each of the suppliers and that score is allocated against each of the criteria from the table in Table 5.1.

Table 5.2 Supplier assessment results

Supplier name	Criteria ID								
	1	2	3	4	5	6	7	8	Total
S Tools	7	6	2	6	2	3	4	4	34
J Web	2	6	2	1	3	3	3	6	26
M Work	1	8	6	3	10	4	3	5	40
Total possible score	10	20	10	10	15	10	10	15	100

The scoring system sets a fixed number of points for any given criterion and this is shown at the bottom of the first column. These points are distributed across the various companies being assessed. This scoring system forces you to make choices over which company is top for each of the given criteria. You can weight the importance of any given criterion by simply allocating a larger number of points. In Table 5.2, criterion 2, criterion 5 and criterion 8 all have a larger point allocation.

This method of appraisal isn't always suitable for assessing suppliers. If the list of suppliers is large it can be difficult to distribute the points in this way. Each of the suppliers can end up with only one point each, making the enforced distribution worthless. When the list of potential suppliers is long it is more effective to use a maximum score system. A maximum score system assigns a maximum value to each of the criteria. However, each company is marked individually and there is no distribution of points between companies. This means that if 10 points are available it is possible for each company to gain 10 points. With this scheme you do not have to worry about keeping within an overall allocation. The obvious difficulty with this scheme is that it does not force you to choose between the companies. This in turn means that there might be little differentiation between the top three or four companies. When this happens you should rescore the companies using the original method.

Handling the chosen outsource company
Once you have decided which external company you would like to use you need to decide on the contract type you want to employ. There are five main contract types that might be employed: fixed price, time and materials, royalty based, partnership or cost plus fixed rewards. Each has a place within the project. Often a combination of contract vehicles will be used.

● *Fixed price*
   Fixed price is one of the most common contract types in projects. A vendor supplies goods or services to the project for a fixed sum of money. In principle this sounds an ideal contract

type. The buying organization states the requirement and then the supplier delivers.

Sadly, few fixed price contracts work as well as the theory suggests they should. To gain an understanding of fixed price contracts you must consider the risks involved in this contract type. Generally in a fixed price contract the supplier shoulders most of the risk. However, the customer (the project in this case) pays for this in the contract price. The supplier charges a premium to the project for the work undertaken. The size of the premium is related to the risk involved. Smart suppliers manage the risks well; they tie down the scope and they deliver according to that scope. This is great for the project as long as the scope doesn't change. However, scope almost always changes, especially with advanced projects. Smart suppliers bid for the work knowing this. They work out what they would like to charge and then they reduce that cost to a minimum in order to win the business. The suppliers do this assuming that they can use the changes that will be required to enable them to make a profit on the project. Thinking of this as an equation helps (see Figure 5.1).

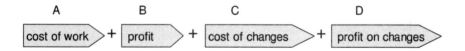

Figure 5.1 Fixed price contract equation

A and B and C will often be very reasonable; D will not be. For example, imagine that the project did not specify a cooker switch for the kitchen. The project remembered the wiring, the hole in the wall and all of the associated work. They simply forgot to specify the switch. The contractor could charge anything it wanted for that cooker switch. This could be very difficult for you if the project was the completion of a new office headquarters. It would be difficult because the project would be unable to complete until the cooker switch was installed. The building would not be fully functional since the cooker would not be working. This would be particularly difficult if it was a building where the kitchen concerned was the staff canteen, especially if the canteen had to serve three meals a day. There are, of course, approaches to dealing with this. For example, you could wait until the end of the project and have the cooker switch put in by another contractor. However, it is likely that there will be many such instances and so it won't be practical always to adopt this approach. A simple way to avoid it is to encourage bidding contractors to limit or cap the price that they will charge. This cap should include a limit on any profit for additional requirements. In this way you gain some level of protection from excessive profiteering.

- *Time and materials*
  Time and materials is possibly the second most commonly used contract vehicle. With this contract type, the project pays a day rate or an hourly rate for resources. In addition to the resource cost the project also pays for the materials used. The materials are charged at cost. This contract vehicle is useful since it allows the organization to change its mind on an ongoing basis. It is generally not excessively expensive to add new requirements to this contract type. This is especially true when compared to fixed price where any change tends to be very expensive.

  Unfortunately organizations often fail with this type of contract to keep the costs under control. Members of the organization often change the requirements. The constant change in requirements drives up the project cost. Care needs to be taken to avoid this.

- *Royalty*
  Unlike the first two contract mechanisms, royalty is the first mechanism where organizations jointly accept the risk involved. Royalty is a method where a supplier organization supplies goods that are paid for on a royalty basis. Royalty-based work normally relies on a volume business proposition. This is shown in Figure 5.2.

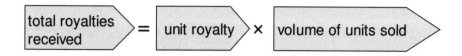

Figure 5.2 Royalty equation

The company supplying goods or services on a royalty basis is normally the one taking the majority of the risk. A graph of the risk helps to explain the situation more clearly (see Figure 5.3).

Until the breakeven point, the supplying organization is assuming the risk for the work. However, after the breakeven point the supplying organization will continue to make profit on an ongoing basis. In negotiating the contract clearly the position of the breakeven point is very important. It needs to end up in a position that both companies are happy with. One method often used to help supplying organizations with this

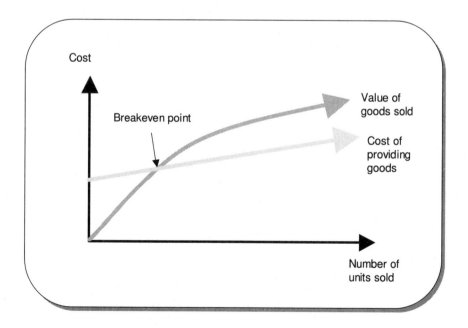

Figure 5.3 Royalty equation graph

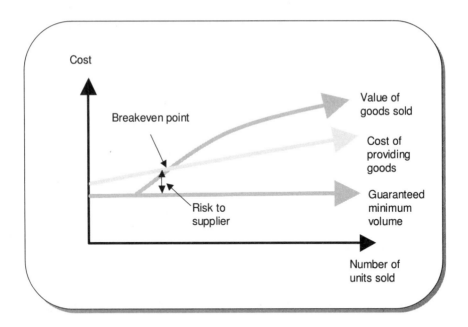

Figure 5.4 Supplier risk

type of contract is the setting of a minimum volume. This minimum volume is normally before the breakeven point but nevertheless it does remove some of the risk for the supplying organization (see Figure 5.4).

● *Partnership*
Partnership is used to mean the sharing of risk. Both parties agree on a business model and then they try jointly to make the model successful. The use of the partnership model depends on the economic climate within which the project has been undertaken. The economic climate is important since it normally dictates the amount of risk that an organization is prepared to take. In poor economic conditions, shared risk is always attractive and as a result organizations are keener to follow the partnership model.

A partnership is generally a combination of two or more contract models. One organization might be willing to undertake some of the work on a fixed price basis and another on a time and materials basis. These two contracts are then joined by the agreement of a business model. This model sets out the profit that each organization expects to make. In general all work on the project is transparent to the partners and is auditable. The partnership almost always includes a section explaining how the contract will be terminated.

- *Cost plus fixed reward*

  The cost plus fixed reward model is when a contracting company supplies everything at cost. In return it gains fixed bonuses, which are paid on the basis of results achieved. Unlike the time and materials contract type, the costs in this contract model are auditable. This means that any costs are the actual costs and it's only these costs that can be sought. This model works by offering suppliers large bonuses for delivering on time. Contracts structured in this manner normally allow bonuses to be paid on delivery or early delivery of goods. Unfortunately when it goes wrong the whole bonus is normally forfeited. When this happens it can be difficult to motivate a supplier. The supplier would prefer to put its staff on other contracts where bonuses are still available.

Common issues with outsource contracts

Before leaving outsource models and considering internal resources there are four other areas that must be considered when dealing with external suppliers. These are change control, schedules, IPR and copyright and trade mark:

- *Change control*

  One of the most important aspects of control in an advanced project is change control. It is important since any change, no matter how small, has some impact on the project. This is particularly true of advanced projects, which generally are trying to deliver something that is not understood. This lack of understanding means that change is inevitable, which results in the need for change control.

  When undertaken properly the change control process can be extremely helpful to the project manager. It ensures that the work being undertaken is understood and controlled. The two most likely sources for initiating change are the commissioning organization and the supplying organization. The commissioning organization, at the start of the project, generally knows the direction it wants to travel in but often it does not know the final destination. The supplying organization wants to supply a good result to its customer. It wants to do this because it would like to be recommended to others to do similar work and also because it would like to be used again by the original commissioning organization. This results in the supplying organization suggesting ways that the project and its result can be improved. It would be easy to believe that the supplying organization only suggests new ideas to enable it to generate more income. However, this is not always the case; frequently, supplying organizations will suggest undertaking additional work at cost or for free. One of the reasons they do this is to generate goodwill and to demonstrate that they are not simply there for the money.

The supplying organization and the sponsoring organization generally have two reasons for change requests. Firstly, there are good ideas that occur to team members. Good ideas tend to happen as the project progresses because the team discover new and different ways of considering tasks. This might involve being able to do something in a cheaper manner or perhaps undertaking work early to reduce risks. A simple illustration might be building an extra room on to a building. Obviously it would be cheaper to do this when the building contractors are still on site rather than to bring building contractors back on site just to build a single room.

Good ideas tend to be more obvious as the project progresses because people start to understand what is going on. It is often very difficult to comprehend the whole picture of an advanced project until it has progressed. Often it's not until the detailed pictures have been developed that ideas start to be generated. Good ideas can be very motivational for team members, especially if they are implemented.

The second reason for change is when the organizations want to sort out poor ideas that have been implemented by the project. Projects always have areas that team members wish were redone. Sometimes they don't get tackled during the project and afterwards people wonder why. Generally it's cheaper to sort out a poor idea when it is first recognized rather than waiting until the end of the project. An argument often used for delaying putting right poorly completed ideas is that it is not motivating for the project team. However, the project team generally are quite perceptive and they recognize poor ideas, and often it is actually motivational for them to see poor ideas being sorted out. You should be conscious of this when considering whether to tackle poorly implemented ideas.

● *Schedules*
One of the key control mechanisms for external consultants or suppliers is the schedule. The schedule is therefore important and so it is often included as part of the contract. Since it forms part of the contract you should have made yourself fully aware of the details of it. An experienced project manager will have ensured that the schedule in the contract is flexible. A flexible schedule is one that does not prescribe everything in detail. To achieve this it should be a milestone-based schedule with checkpoints. This would be similar to the macro plan.

You should ensure that the schedule, like all baseline documents, is included in the project's change control system. This means that any proposed change to it will need to be ratified prior to the change being made. This will help to protect the project from suppliers simply undertaking work that they have discussed at meetings but that has not been formally agreed.

● *IPR*
Intellectual property rights are the rights that an organization asserts over its ideas. These ideas are often the subject of a patent. The patent explains in broad terms the idea that the

organization wishes to protect. Project managers and other senior managers often think of patents as things to be protected. They believe that companies will use them to stop others using the organization's ideas. However, the opposite is often true. Companies are happy and encourage others to exploit their ideas. They use patents as the vehicle to ensure that they are paid for their use.

● *Copyright and trade mark*
Copyright and trade mark are ways of protecting the visual images that an organization feels define its worth. They are often applied to organization logos. Project managers can and often do fail to consider their implications. For an organization, the copyright and trade mark issues are normally very important. Project managers therefore need to have a good awareness at all times of the use of protected material. For example, they may want to display a British Standards logo to show quality approval.

The issues with IPR and copyright and trade mark are very complex and vary widely from project to project. They need careful consideration and normally they need legal advice. You simply need to be aware that there is a potential problem and then need to be sure that the problem is addressed in any outsource contract.

Handling the internal resources

In parallel to deciding about the external resources you need to consider how you will handle the internal resources in a mixed project. Internal resources require you to undertake either a development strategy or a monitoring strategy.

Development

A development strategy simply means that the resources within an organization do not have the skills level required to meet the needs of the project. In extreme cases there may be no suitable resources within the organization. Despite the lack of skills the organization may still decide that internal resources must be used. If this happens then you will need to find a method to develop the required resources inside of the organization. In most cases this will mean you relying on your work package managers for help.

Developing the resources in-house normally involves building a training programme. This programme should be centred on the work required to complete the advanced project. In some large organizations the personnel or human resources departments can help. Whoever sets up the training for the project personnel should focus first on understanding the skills required and secondly on having suitable courses. You must remember that if you are building the resources inside the organization it is likely that there will be a long-term requirement for the resource. So you must make sure that whatever training programme is developed it accounts for the organization's long-term need.

Monitoring

A monitoring strategy for internal resources is simply continuously checking that project team members are performing the necessary skills at an appropriate level. Much of this is achieved through the mechanisms explained in Chapter 6, which describes project control. These almost always relate to finding suitable metrics that can be used to monitor the work involved, for example the number of work hours spent. If you discover a problem then you will need to adopt the development approach.

WHAT IS THE STRATEGY FOR THE EXECUTION OF YOUR PROJECT?

Once you understand the type of project and the way it will be staffed, you need to create a strategy for its execution. This strategy will bring together all the pieces of the complex jigsaw that you have worked on so far. If it is prepared effectively then the strategy will express clearly how the project is going to use the resources available to it to achieve the project goals. Since advanced projects normally have a large scale and scope it is necessary to write the strategy in a summary format. The summary should cover the resource needs and deployment for the four fundamental building blocks of projects:

- scope;
- quality;
- resource;
- timescale.

The strategy needs to cover each of these areas from two perspectives. Firstly, it needs to cover the short-term or the tactical work and, secondly, it needs to cover the long-term or the strategic work.

Scope

By this phase of the project the scope should be properly understood. The planning should be in place and a macro plan ought to have been published. This plan should explain what will happen and when it is going to happen. It is possible that at this stage some of the detailed descriptions for the work may still be incomplete. This is only likely to affect work planned to start more than six months in the future. This lack of planning for some of the work means that the strategy needs to cover both the known scope and the unknown scope.

Strategy for known scope

Many project managers find it odd that a strategy is required for scope that is understood. When the scope is understood it is likely that there will be a good understanding of the method that will be used to deliver it. This means that detailed plans can be produced, negating the need for strategy. For most project types this logic is probably true. However, advanced projects are not like other projects. The only certainty that you have in an advanced project is that everything is going to change. This is the nature of advanced projects. The work is normally new, it probably has not been tried before and it is often unknown whether it will be fit for its intended purpose. Often the sponsoring organization does not know what it is that it wants to achieve. It only knows a general direction in which it wants to go. For example, an organization may want to build a new headquarters. The organization may only know that it wants to make it an exciting space for its employees. It may have no idea what this really means but as the project progresses it may discover new ideas that it wants to include. As a result it may want to change direction.

This background of constant change is very important to recognize. The execution strategy is the method that you have for dealing with the constant change. It is this strategy that will ensure that the project will progress smoothly, quickly and easily. The strategy is the simple way of understanding where the project should have reached and at what time it should have reached it.

To build a great strategy you need to look at the overall project. Perhaps the simplest way of achieving this is to start with the macro plan that you have already put together. This plan already defines many of the meaningful points that are going to occur on the journey to the end of the project. These points are a great starting place for defining the known scope strategy. For the strategy to be successful it needs to avoid falling into the common trap of being too detailed. It needs to remain abstracted from the detail. This ensures that people reading the strategy, or following the strategy, are able to understand where they have reached at any particular moment. A good metric for the strategy is whether it can be written on to one or two sides of A4 or A3 paper. Generally speaking, if the strategy cannot be condensed into a small amount of space then it's too complicated. The strategy needs to be written in a manner that enables one person to understand all of it in one reading.

It can be tempting for a project manager simply to take the existing macro plan and rewrite parts of it from a new perspective. It is tempting to take the detailed milestone plan and simply write down the milestones and say 'This is our strategy.' Whilst doing either of these things will speed up the production of the execution strategy they will not help you manage the project effectively. If you adopt either of these quick production methods then you should also accept that your execution strategy is worthless.

The strategy needs to be broad and high-level in its definition and its presentation. Perhaps a simple example of a strategy statement might be:

- In Q1 the foundation will be laid and all major ground works will be completed.
- In Q2 the framework will be erected, the cladding attached and the building made watertight.
- In Q3 the internal fit-out of the building will be completed and the power and services made available.
- In Q4 the building will be commissioned with all necessary equipment to allow it to work properly.

This short series of bullet points explains the complete strategy for getting a building constructed, fitted out and into operational use. Obviously there will be a large number of tasks that need to be executed successfully to achieve this work. These tasks will require a substantial amount of planning to enable the building to be built, the framework to be erected, the cladding to be put in place and so on. Designs would need to be agreed for the foundations, the steelwork, the mechanical systems, the electrical systems and so on. However, although all of these plans and designs are needed, they are not required for the strategy. The short paragraph with the four bullet points clearly explains to anyone the major stages of the building project.

As the project progresses you should continuously refer to this strategy. There is a clear objective for every quarter and a clear way of determining whether the objective for that quarter has been met. This makes it reasonably simple for you to determine if the project has remained on track and whether it is likely to achieve its overall objective. For example, perhaps at the end of Q1 the foundations have not been laid and the major ground works have not been completed. It would be reasonable for you to assume that the project is falling behind schedule. If the work still has not been completed by the end of Q2 then you would know that the project is in trouble.

Execution strategy is not only useful for assessing the current work. It also allows you to assess the future work. It sets out potential areas that should be examined for long-lead items that may need to be addressed early in the project. This enables you to anticipate work that needs to be undertaken early in order to achieve success. For example, the frame of the building may take many months to design and to get manufactured, especially if the frame of the building is unusual. You could anticipate this need from reviewing the strategy.

Strategy for the unknown scope

Once the strategy for the known scope has been defined you should centre your attention on the unknown scope. It is frequently believed that it will be difficult to define the strategy for the unknown scope. Since the scope is not clear, project managers often believe that a strategy cannot be created. However, defining the strategy for the unknown scope is not significantly different to defining the strategy for the known scope. The solution to understanding the unknown scope is to define what you don't know. Once you've defined what you don't know then it is possible to decide what needs to be done to define it. This can be simply achieved by completing a table that has different columns listing out the unknown scope, what's not understood about the scope and when it needs to be resolved. An example table is shown in Table 5.3.

Table 5.3 shows four columns. The first column sets out the unknown scope for a particular item. The second column explains what needs to be clarified about the scope and the third column sets out the timescale that you have in which to resolve the points for clarification. Filling in a table like this will help you to focus

Table 5.3 Unknown scope definition

Unknown scope description	Points to be clarified	Timescale for resolution	Comments
Size of code footprint	RAM available on device Architecture of device	RAM usage 3 weeks Architecture 1 week	Can make some basic assumptions that others will have to live with
UI design	What interactions are required	Prior to code work starting End of Q1	Basic UI can be created without the design, allowing work to progress

on the unknown issues. Often you will find that there are only a few unknowns. Frequently the initial table will include a large number of items. However, an early review will quickly reduce the number included to a few key items of unknown scope. Once the key items have been identified they should be built into a strategy similar in manner to the one for the known scope. For example:

- In Q2 the operating system including its version needs to be defined and agreed.
- In Q3 the hardware needs to be selected and work on its integration needs to start.

You should now be in the position to write down two strategy expressions: one for the known scope and one for the unknown scope. Once this has been achieved you should be in a strong position to identify future scope issues. By being able to identify upcoming issues you should be able to reduce the risk on the project significantly. However, despite the benefit of this scope statement you must undertake other work before you can define the execution strategy of the project. A series of bullet points covering scope is not a project execution strategy. Clearly the other fundamental areas of the project need to be covered if the full strategic intent of the advanced project is to be conveyed.

Quality

Most project managers understand the need for quality and the need for a quality outcome from their project. However, many don't really understand the details of how quality is achieved. As a consequence of poor understanding, project managers are unable to guide and coach others in quality issues. This results in a general lack of understanding, which extends throughout the project. When this poor understanding exists, a clearly thought-through strategy for quality is unlikely to be in place. When this is the case you need to take immediate action. A well-thought-through quality strategy should be central to the project if a quality outcome is to be achieved. It is important that you take time to educate yourself sufficiently about quality to ensure that you are able to teach other people.

The first step in defining a clear quality strategy is to understand what is intended by quality. A common mistake in trying to understand quality is trying to define it in a broad manner, for example 'We won't be satisfied until our customers are.' Whilst this is a great objective it is unlikely to help in the practical realization of quality. Sadly it is common for projects to take on such a statement as a way of introducing quality. You tell everyone in your team that once the customer is happy then you will be happy too. Unfortunately this way almost always fails. The customer rarely ends up happy. This approach is sometimes called the 'general statement approach'. It is achieved by simply stating a general ethos for quality. Sadly most of these statements are too abstract for project team members. Examples of general statements are:

● 'Quality comes at a price but it's a price worth paying.'
● 'We will always strive to do our best – quality is important.'
● 'Quality must be at the heart of our work.'
● 'We measure our success by the quality of our product.'

Although these statements may inspire team members they don't actually tell them what they should do. Instead quality should be undertaken as a targeted activity. This means identifying specific tasks within the project that the organization is going to undertake. Targeting quality in this way, for a specific project task, ensures that it becomes measurable and useful to the people concerned. The easiest way to define quality for a project is to assess how you would measure whether the project has succeeded or failed. Effectively this is the definition of the mission statement of the project. Some examples might be:

● 'End consumers are delighted with their new phone.'
● 'The staff love their new working environment.'

- 'The software never fails.'
- 'Customers are breaking down our door trying to buy our product.'

These four examples are very different in nature. However, they do have a common theme and that is defining what a successful project outcome might be. Examining the project from the end user's point of view, that is the customer's point of view, enables the quality criteria to be clearly and easily defined. However, these statements are not sufficient on their own to merit a quality strategy. They need to be broken down into manageable steps that allow implementation.

None of the example statements will be able to help an individual team member with the implementation of quality. Questions will be raised immediately such as 'How can a simple strategy statement predict whether a consumer will be delighted?' Another question might be 'How can you determine whether the staff loved your environment?' Put simply, a quality statement can't answer either of these questions directly. Instead the quality statement must try to assess the characteristics needed to resolve these questions. Once the characteristics are defined then the strategy can set out how to achieve the characteristics.

Defining the characteristics is achieved by looking for certain features. This is achieved by asking three simple questions. These questions aim to understand the fundamental issues with project quality. They are:

- Who are the judges of quality?
- How will they judge the quality?
- Is their judgement measurable?

The first two of these are reasonably easy to determine. For example, for the first quality statement it is the phone customers and their delight that count. The third question however, 'Is their judgement measurable?', is a much harder question to address. You need to spend time assessing what customer delight is. It is possible to achieve this through techniques such as focus groups. Even if focus groups cannot be run it is still possible for you to gather trusted opinions to enable them to make an assessment.

You should spend some time with appropriate team members trying to answer each of the three questions. For each of the questions you should try to produce detailed answers. These answers should then relate to the original project quality statement. Wherever possible you and your supporting team should split the answers into chunks of time. Each chunk of time should have a measurable outcome associated with it. Once all the questions have been answered you need finally to set out a quality strategy. The strategy should be set out in a similar manner to that for scope. For example:

- In Q2 the key characteristics that will delight the customers will be defined.
- In Q3 the characteristics that will delight the customers will be checked by using a focus group.
- In Q4 the first sample product will be put to the focus group and remedial action taken depending on the feedback from the focus group.
- In Q1 the final product will be measured against the characteristics defined at the start of the project, that is the characteristics that you believe will delight the customers.

This completed statement can then be added to the scope statement. The next area to examine in producing the execution strategy is resource.

Resource

A well-designed resource strategy should enable you to achieve your goal. A badly defined resource strategy is likely to give significant problems. Often project managers controlling advanced projects don't bother defining a resource strategy. They mistakenly believe that the detailed work package plans will serve as protection against resource problems.

To get a sufficient overview of the resources needed, you need to revisit the macro plan. In the macro plan resources were examined from a summary level. They were broken into chunks and those chunks were defined on a time basis, perhaps quarterly. These figures should now be used and assessed against certain criteria. You should decide the criteria specific to your project. However, some useful guidance criteria are listed below:

- Are the macro plan estimates still correct when taking into account the detailed plans?
- Do the macro plan estimates explain what skill sets will be needed to deliver the plan?
- Is there training in place to make sure the plan will work? If there isn't training in place, is the training clearly identified?
- Are the resources available in-house or are they going to be sourced externally?
- Do the resource plans take into account the need of the scope strategy and the quality strategy?

With answers to these questions it's possible to start to pull together a resource strategy. As with the quality and scope strategies, the resource strategy should be succinct and time-bound. It is difficult to be prescriptive about the strategy statement since advanced projects vary so much in scope. However, it is possible to design a basic formula that can be changed, dependent on circumstances:

In quarter X resources will be required with the following skills:

- At least YY people will be required.
- A ZZ proportion of the work will be resourced using staff external to the organization.

Obviously the blanks should be replaced with actual figures. An example statement might be:

In Q1 resources will be required: general labourers, architects, clerk of works. At least 20 people will be needed: 15 labourers, 4 architects, 1 clerk of works. All labourers will be sourced from outside of the organization.

This resource statement should now be added to the scope statement and the quality statement. This should result in three chunks of strategy that all relate to one another.

Timescale

As with resource, a timescale strategy might seem an odd concept. Again it is easy to believe that the detailed plans will define the time line sufficiently. Whilst this is true to an extent it is only part of the overall picture. It is equally important to understand the main milestones in a simple fashion. This high-level picture helps to keep the project understandable. And indeed this time-bound method is already part of the three strategy statements that have been defined.

The first step in defining a timescale strategy is to gather together the main milestones. These are easily identified from the work packages. A simple list can prove to be effective and helpful here (see Table 5.4).

Table 5.4 has four columns. The first column is the milestone column and this should be populated with all of the main project milestones. The second column contains the title of the work package that the milestone is attached to. In some cases a milestone may be attached to several work packages; when this happens the prime work package should be chosen. The third column is the due date column and should be the planned date, not the planned date plus contingency. The final column is included to allow for comments to be added. The table should be populated with all of the major milestones within the project.

Table 5.4 Timescale strategy definition

Milestone	Work package	Due date	Comments
M1: Alpha delivered	Development of Application package 1	Week 4 (end of)	Functionality required is defined in project plan
M2: Beta delivered	Development of Application package 1	Week 25 (end of)	All functionality to be included although may not be debugged fully
M3: Release candidate	Development of Application package 1	Week 40 (end of)	Fully tested software

Some project planning tools allow the creation of this table in an automated manner.

Once the table has been completed it is likely that there will be groups of milestones. If the list is constructed in a spreadsheet package it can be easily sorted. This makes finding the groups simple. The first column to sort by is the date. Once sorted by the date, the next step is to pick out some groupings. The simplest way is to start by dividing the total milestones in any one year by four. For example, 16 milestones in a 12-month period would be split into four groups of milestones with four milestones in each group. All milestone groups, once identified, should be examined to identify whether they are similar in nature. If they are then this should be used as a project group. If they are not then they should be moved between groups until a logical breakdown is achieved. The objective behind splitting the year into four is to enable you to build a quarterly statement. This type of statement is useful since it is easily remembered. Q1 is easier to remember than May to August.

You should now create a quarterly statement that covers the time line of the project. This should be similar to the previous strategy statements for scope, quality and resources. For example:

- In Q1 the project milestones M1 to M3 will be met.
- In Q2 the project milestones M4 to M9 will be met.

Once this statement is ready you are in a position to create the overall execution strategy for the project.

Creating the overall execution strategy

Creating the overall execution strategy is initially a relatively mechanistic process. You take the four separate strategy statements and combine them. This is simply achieved by using the cut-and-paste function on a word-processing package. You should resist the temptation to break apart the strategies or to rewrite them into one concise statement. Although this would make the strategy simpler to remember it would also reduce its impact. By not combining the statements you avoid any dilution of the intended message.

Once the mechanistic joining together of the strategies has been completed you must take time to build them into one presentable document. This means adding some basic explanatory text to expand bullet points that may not be obvious. The document should be no more than 2,000 words. Assuming there are 300 words on a page, this results in a strategy document that should be completed in seven pages including diagrams. Keeping the document short and succinct improves its readability and helps to ensure that busy senior managers will be able to find time to read it.

Once completed, the document should be presented initially to the project steering group and then to the key project stakeholders. The stakeholders should be gathered together and the contents of the document presented. The meeting should be followed by a question-and-answer session and finally the distribution of the project strategy document. The completed strategy should be updated and redistributed on a regular basis. If the strategy has been written using a quarterly timescale then updating on a quarterly basis would be a reasonable target. For shorter projects, months may have been used and therefore perhaps a monthly update would be sensible. In all cases you should use your judgement when deciding how often to update the strategy.

HOW WILL YOU IMPLEMENT THE EXECUTION STRATEGY?

An execution strategy is useless unless it is implemented and where possible adhered to. To achieve this, you must use a systematic method. The strategy created so far has been long-term or strategic in its presentation. It presents the project and its need at an overview or summary level only. To allow the strategy to be implemented it needs to be translated into a detailed or tactical execution method. It is this tactical execution method that will allow you to deliver the overall strategy successfully. There are many methods that can be used but generally they can be categorized into one of the following groups:

- waterfall;
- time box;
- light method;
- formal method;
- rolling wave.

Waterfall

Waterfall is a technique that is commonly applied on software projects. However, the underlying method can be applied to any project type. As its name implies, waterfall is a method that starts at the beginning of the project and then continues in an uninterrupted manner until the end. This is illustrated in Figure 5.5.

Figure 5.5 shows the process of taking a requirement through to the final test of the built product. Different waterfall methods have different names for the phases but they all work on the same principle. Each phase in the waterfall has to complete before the next phase can start. This means that there is no returning from the design phase to the requirements phase; each phase is distinct. The transition between the phases is often managed by using a technique call 'gates'. The gate is a representation for the passage between one phase and the next. In the waterfall method, the gates are one-way gates. This implies that, once a gate has been passed, the project cannot return to the work that was being carried out prior to passing through the gate. This can make it difficult to pass through gates.

This method works well for projects (or parts of projects) that are well defined, for example building a new house. In this example the project requirements and delivery method are probably well defined. This understanding will be achieved because the builders have done the same work many times before. In this

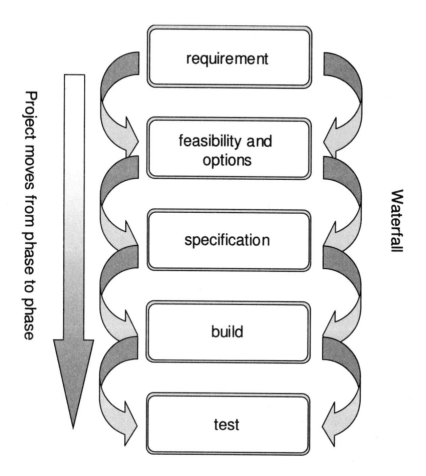

Figure 5.5 Waterfall model

illustration the use of project gates can be very effective since it's very clear what should have happened at each stage, for example the foundations must be poured or the building must be watertight.

Unfortunately this method is not appropriate in advanced projects. Advanced projects are rarely well defined. It is very rare for them to have a solid measurable output at any moment in time. However, the technique should not be disregarded completely. It is likely that some parts of the project will be able to use the technique.

Time box

The time box technique is used extensively in projects. However, both inexperienced and experienced project managers frequently fail to recognize that the technique is being used. This can mean that project managers fail to gain all of the potential benefits. This can be overcome simply. Project managers need only gain a basic understanding of the technique to enable them to know when it is being used and when to use it.

In simple language, a time box is a method whereby a poorly understood task is broken into a series of more manageable chunks. Often it involves gathering together people involved in the tasks and asking them to define short-term goals. The goals, once reached, are then reappraised and a new set of goals defined.

Time boxing can be achieved by following five straightforward steps.

- *Step 1*
  Define a short-term time horizon, normally about one month.
- *Step 2*
  Set clear, measurable objectives for that time horizon.
- *Step 3*
  Select the appropriate team and gather them together.
- *Step 4*
  Get the team to work towards the objective. Ensure that they understand what needs to be achieved by the end of the time box.
- *Step 5*
  At the end of the time horizon, or the time box, assess the result. If the overall objective has not been achieved, set a new time box, beginning again at step 1.

Although the steps are reasonably self-explanatory, it is worth expanding on two of them: step 1, the time horizon; and step 3, the pulling together of the time box team.

Step 1, the defining of a short-term time horizon

The time horizon is defined by thinking about the whole task. Once you understand the whole task you should break it into manageable chunks. These chunks are what sets the time box size for the task. All of the chunks do not need to be planned in detail. Only the current time chunk needs to be planned in detail.

Figure 5.6 shows the time boxing method in action. There are two iterations in Figure 5.6. The first iteration shows the total task broken into three chunks. Each chunk has been defined as being the same size and taking an equal amount of time. Once the initial split has been made, task 1 is planned in detail and the other tasks set aside. As the work progresses, the first time box completes. As it completes you should start to assess task 2. With the additional knowledge gained through completing task 1 you are able to assess that you need to split task 2 into two time boxes. This is a normal result of the time box process. As work progresses, understanding improves and as a result plans also improve. Eventually you will progress on to task 3 and complete the project work.

One of the key advantages of time boxing is the short-term focus it provides. Instead of team members worrying about how to complete difficult tasks they focus solely on short-term goals. This focus helps progress since time is not spent on planning activities that are not understood.

Step 3, the pulling together of the time box team

Gathering together the right team is an essential part of time boxing. The team needs to be composed of people who have authority to make decisions on behalf of the organization. For example, the person who is dealing with requirements should be able to decide whether something can be left out of the work or not. This principle of empowerment of the team needs to underpin all of those who are team members. They need to believe that they have the support to make things happen.

Time boxing is a method that is commonly used for advanced projects since the requirements are often unclear. As a method it

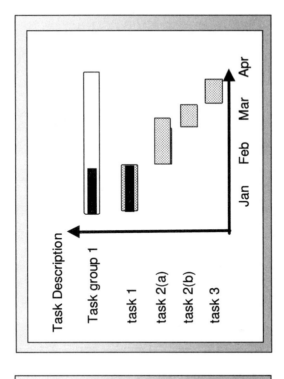

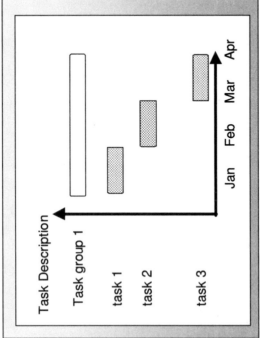

Figure 5.6 Time box

provides an excellent way of moving quickly through difficult and uncharted territory. One of the reasons that time box works well as a technique is the short cycle time for requirements definition.

Light projects

Unlike the previous two ways of working, this technique is not strictly a technique or a method. Instead it is a way of thinking about projects. This technique simply involves ruthlessly removing parts of the project process that are not useful. This removal is carried out regardless of the quality system and the organizational procedures.

Most projects that are advanced in nature attract significant amounts of bureaucracy. The overhead associated with bureaucracy can cause significant difficulties for project managers. Although they may try to support the quality system continually, sometimes the paperwork involved becomes too much. This tends to be especially true for inexperienced project managers. Their inexperience leads them to rely on processes. They hope that the processes will support them and help them avoid making mistakes. The consequence of this is that they can end up undertaking a significant amount of process in the project that a more experienced project manager would disregard. In many instances a heavily bureaucratic system is not appropriate and should not be used.

Although it is tempting simply to throw away processes, this is not a wise course of action. In all cases caution should be used when considering the removal of bureaucracy. Ideally a risk assessment should be undertaken before the decision to stop following a process is made for any given task. The assessment should have two parts to it. Firstly, it should examine whether the task concerned has been undertaken before. This assessment should be carried out by you or the work package manager for the task. Secondly, the assessment should examine whether the organization has a history of completing tasks like the one being assessed. This can be achieved by providing an analogy assessment (see Chapter 2). If after analysing the task you are confident that the organization is not at substantial risk then you should consider using a cut-down or light method of project management.

To introduce a light method of project management, you must first decide what actual technique you are going to use. Once you have decided your technique you then need to break your technique into its constituent parts and assess each part in turn. For example, if you are going to use a waterfall technique then you should examine each phase in turn. You should assess whether the phase is actually required. If it is not then it should be set aside for that task. Once you have decided what to drop from the technique you should record this in a plan. Normally this plan is the quality plan for the project. If the light thinking method is applied effectively then it will result in a reduced amount of work.

Formal

Not surprisingly formal project management is the opposite of light project management. With this method everything is documented in great detail. Using a detailed method is appropriate in many types of project. For example, nuclear work or air traffic control work requires detailed control of every project aspect.

This method is really the application of a chosen technique to its fullest extent. In practice this will occur mainly in government-funded projects. It happens with these projects because funding can be made available for the amount of work involved. It's worth noting that it is required for these projects because of the safety critical nature of the project. As with the light method, the important part of this method is the understanding of what is actually needed. The objective for you is to recognize that there is a requirement for this method. This means recognizing that the organization that is undertaking the project is looking for a particular way of working. Once the particular method of working has been identified you simply need to apply it.

Rolling wave

The rolling wave method is similar to time boxing. It uses the same principle of splitting the work into different areas. The principal difference between the time box technique and the rolling wave technique is the focus of each box. In rolling wave there are simply two boxes. The first box is approximately three months long and is the detail of the work to be undertaken. The other box is the rest of the project. The technique is illustrated in Figure 5.7.

The rolling wave is a method of splitting the project in two. The first part is the tactical part of the project and the second part the strategic part of the project. The rolling wave method should be used on any project of one year or greater in duration. The rolling wave technique is applied at a higher level than time boxing. Therefore rolling wave would cover many activities, as opposed to time boxing, which would cover only one activity. Rolling wave would normally be used at a higher level for the general management of the project. It would not be used for the management of an individual task within the project. Individual tasks would be managed by time boxes.

Whatever technique you adopt for implementing the strategy of the project, it is essential that it is supportive of the ideal of a quality output.

HOW CAN YOU ENSURE THAT QUALITY REMAINS ON THE AGENDA?

'Quality requirements have been woven through the material in this book.' This simple statement might not seem particularly important. However, it demonstrates an attitude to quality that all project managers should adopt. Quality needs to be built into the project, not bolted on as an afterthought. Building quality in can be a difficult concept but it doesn't have to be. Understanding what is meant by quality is something that project managers often fail to do. Quality is simply something doing what it is supposed

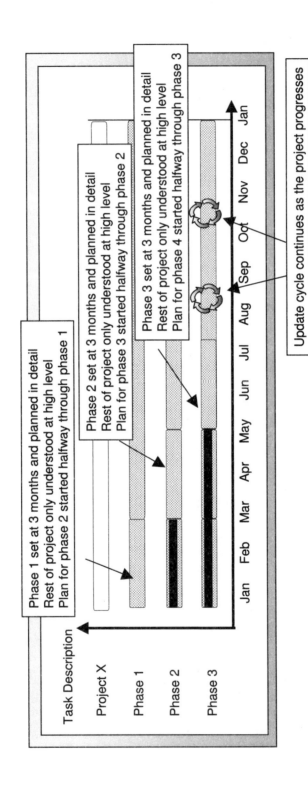

Figure 5.7 Rolling wave

to do. Sadly, quality is frequently thought of only as an abstract concept. It is described as something that you intuitively know is there. For most project managers it is something that's not really being measured. As noted in the definition of the strategy for quality, this is not an acceptable position for you as the manager of an advanced project to adopt. Quality is measurable, it is tangible and it is achievable.

Quality can be achieved partly by using good processes. Processes spell out how tasks should be undertaken and ideally they set the minimum level of quality to be achieved. However, this is only half of the story. Perhaps the more important part is the passion that the project team need. The team need to have a passion if they are to end up with a quality product. Passion is a culture within an organization and it should be built into the fabric of how the advanced project operates. Those in the project should be striving to achieve their best work at all times. You must lead this passionate charge from within the project. This is especially true for an advanced project. The passion must come from the very top.

In practical terms, passion means that it is vital that you pick up on all aspects of poor quality. You must pick up every detail of the project and demand the best from the team. This covers everything including, for example, the quality of the prose within the project documents. For instance, project managers should send back for revision documents that are poorly laid out and difficult to read. They should do this even if the content of the material is correct and acceptable. They must set high standards in everything if they are to ensure that a quality product will be achieved. Although this may seem petty to the project team member concerned, it forces the person to understand that you care about the detail.

Adopting a mindset that demands high quality means that you must find within yourself a passion for the project. You need a passion for excellence in everything. You must have a passion for every deliverable of the project. You must learn to express shock at being offered poor work. It is, after all, through your actions that others will take their lead. If you pick up on poor work then the work package managers will pick up on poor work and so on down the chain. This attitude will result in a culture shift; team members will hesitate before considering presenting poor work. The project team will come to understand that work that is presented must be of a good standard. The culture of the project will demand it.

Demanding high quality at all times can cause problems. The project team slow down their rate of progress as they adjust to the new culture. Deliveries start to slip and a momentum begins whose objective is to lower the quality standard. Those pushing for the drop in the quality standard say that they are addressing the best interests of the project. All they will claim to care about is the pursuit of the more important goal of project delivery. You must not waver. You must make it clear that you expect high-quality work the first time that the work is undertaken. In a few cases this may mean extending timescales to raise the standard of quality. However, this should be the exception rather than the rule. If work is of a high standard then normally the overall timescale falls.

To help the staff with quality issues you can introduce some form of support mechanism. It can be complex or simple. A complex mechanism tends to be bureaucratic in nature. It will involve audits and it will also involve significant paperwork. Surprisingly these bureaucratic systems do have a place in advanced projects. They can be especially useful in safety-critical projects such as aircraft design and build. They can be just as effective as using a simple structure. Whatever you choose to do you should always remember that the key to successful quality is the culture of the project. When a project organization has a strong quality culture it will produce a quality product regardless of the supporting systems.

Commercially available standards

A system that supports the activities of the project effectively can prove invaluable. Whilst it is possible to achieve a quality result through culture alone, it is a difficult route to follow. A system or standard will almost always help in the pursuit of quality. Standards are generally put in place by an organization in a response to a drive to improve quality. There are two commonly used approaches. The first approach is to hire an external organization that is asked to deploy a proprietary quality system. The second approach is to grow organically a series of in-house standards.

Generally organizations switch between organic growth and external systems on an ongoing basis. In practice this does not matter since the two approaches end up with the same result. Often they also achieve the same time frame. This can be modelled in a simple fashion as shown in Figure 5.8.

In the first approach the organization realizes that it isn't possible simply to buy in a system of standards. When it realizes this it switches to using in-house people and gains ownership of the system. Frequently organizations spend a substantial amount of funding on external consultancies in reaching this conclusion. Sadly this makes them wary of using external advice and as a result they struggle to make their own systems work.

In the second approach the organization realizes there are whole areas that it hasn't tackled. It realizes that it needs a structured framework. When it realizes this it turns to help from an outside company. In this case the organization believes that it has wasted substantial amounts of time on internal work. It wrongly blames its internal staff for failing to achieve deployment in a fast timescale.

In practice the organization is swinging between the two approaches. Neither approach on its own is sufficient. Instead the organization needs to use both approaches. A simple model illustrates this (see Figure 5.9).

Practically this means that you need to apply common sense to any quality system that will be used for standards introduction and improvement. Perhaps one of the more helpful ways of ensuring you are able to cope is to understand the main external quality systems that exist. Discovering and understanding these, however, would prove to be impossible if every external system

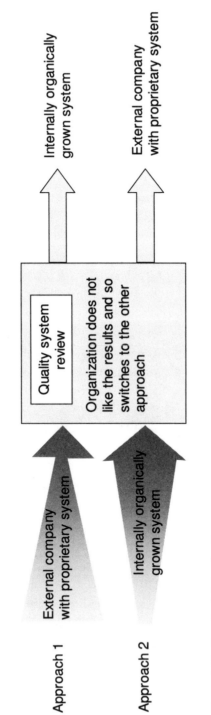

Figure 5.8 Standards introduction

Internally organically grown system

External company with proprietary system

Quality system review

Organization does not like the results and so switches to the other approach

External company with proprietary system

Internally organically grown system

Approach 1

Approach 2

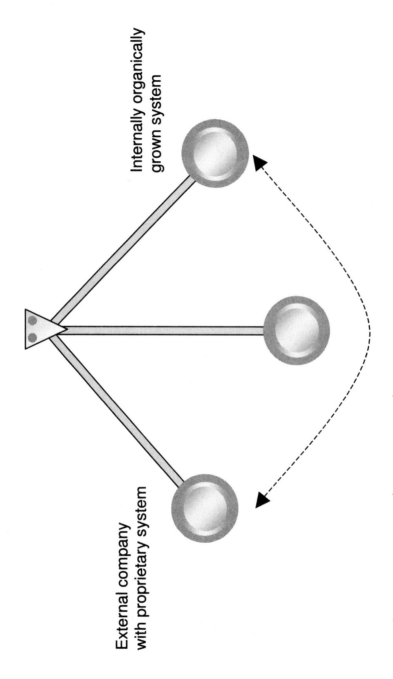

Figure 5.9 Organization swinging between approaches

Internally organically
grown system

External company
with proprietary system

needed to be known. There are many systems that have been published. These range from extremely complex and large systems to very small and focused systems. To overcome this difficulty it's best to know a little bit about some of the most popular systems in use. The most popular systems are probably the capability maturity model (CMM), ISO9000, BS5750, IPMA and PRINCE. All of these systems are readily explained in various textbooks. Basic understanding of them can be achieved by simple research on the Internet.

HAVE YOU ENSURED THAT THOSE INVOLVED CLEARLY UNDERSTAND THEIR ROLE?

As the advanced project moves into its execution phase the roles and responsibilities of its principals need to change. The main principals remain the same: the line manager, the project manager, the work package manager, the sponsor, the customer, partners, suppliers and team members. All of these people need to change their mindset to become delivery focused. This reassessment should be a deliberate move by the people involved in the project. It is helpful for you to sit down with the key individuals and ask them to assess whether they are the right type of person for this stage in the project. You need to explain that the project is moving out of its methodical planning stage. You must ensure that the principals understand that the work is moving from the design phase into the implementation phase. Everyone needs to switch into a delivery mode rather than a planning mode. Principals need to appreciate that they will now be expected just to get on with it regardless of the problems that they encounter.

Being delivery focused means knocking barriers down. Barriers are perceived problems that stand in the way of things being delivered. A common problem is that people feel they do not have the authority to do something or say something. Delivery-focused people tend not to think in those terms. There's a saying, 'Ask for forgiveness, not permission', and this would be a mantra for delivery-focused people. They go with the direction of the plan, looking for the next milestone. These people tend to be very tactical in nature, just going for the next milestone, rather than worrying about the whole picture.

In this phase people need to be very thick-skinned and robust because they will come in for enormous criticism as things progress. This criticism tends to come from people who are not involved in the main delivery process and tends to be in questions such as 'Why was this not planned more effectively?' and so on. At this stage though, the team effort is all-important. The team members, the workers, are the key to success and this means that you should focus on moving the hurdles that may exist out of their way. You should remain focused on the processes and the deliveries that are required and ensure that the reporting is run effectively and the other supporting mechanisms for the team members are in place, for example the defect recording and control method or the scheduling of activities.

Ensuring that the principals understand that they need to adopt this way of working is very important. Talking to the individuals about what will be required in a candid manner offers them the opportunity to assess whether they are suitable for this phase of the work. It also offers a good vehicle for you to open the discussion with the principals about whether they are the right people. The majority of the conversations will result in the principal and you agreeing that the principal should remain in the role. Occasionally people will see that the role is not really for them.

Once you have talked to the principals about their roles you should start to work with the work package managers on building up the teams and their methods of working through this phase. You should remember that project success will not be achieved without a successful team being formed. The team members need to understand what contribution they are expected to make and how to make it.

An effective way to encourage a team approach is to hold team meetings. At these meetings the individual team members get a chance to meet others in the project and hear about progress. If the team meetings are well managed, the team members will leave the meeting feeling motivated and excited. Deciding on the number and structure for team meetings will depend on the size of the project. You should take a number of factors into account:

- *How experienced is the project team?*
  An inexperienced team will need to spend more time together than an experienced one. This experience should be judged both in terms of knowledge to perform tasks and in terms of time spent as part of a team.
- *How distributed is the project team?*
  A distributed team generally requires a more formal structure than one that is co-located. A team that is spread out geographically should have clear and regular meetings in place. This is particularly important if the team is spread across multiple time zones.
- *How mature are the project processes?*
  Advanced projects tend to be undertaken infrequently, since they are expensive and disruptive to the organization. Support in the form of processes for these projects is generally immature. Often the processes are simply the existing project management processes, which are generally inadequate. Where the processes are poor, more structure is required, at least initially, to allow team members to sort out activities and interfaces.

Once you have considered the factors governing what team meetings are required you need to decide on the type of meetings that should be held. There are various categories of meetings:

- *Technical meetings*
  These are held to discuss technical issues. For example, a software project may have an ongoing technical architecture meeting that occurs monthly.

- *Briefing meetings*
  These are held to release information about progress versus plan. This type of meeting should be held regularly to ensure that team members are kept up to date about progress towards the final project goals.
- *Fun events*
  These are held to boost morale. Fun events should be held irregularly but not so irregularly that people are unable to remember the last event. Fun events are often held when a major milestone is passed or a major contract signed.
- *Management meetings*
  Management meetings are held to plan project activities and ensure that the future tactical and strategic plans are acceptable.
- *Customer meetings*
  Meetings with customers are held regularly to explain progress towards key milestones in the project. These can be held with internal or external customers.
- *Supplier meetings*
  These are held with people supplying goods and services. Often these meetings are held with external organizations but they can be held between different divisions of the same organization.

This list of meeting types and factors to consider can seem daunting. Project managers often start out with good intentions about setting up meeting structures. Unfortunately their good intentions often falter when they start to understand the large number of meetings and factors that need to be accounted for. They switch to an abdication mode where they let the meetings form on an as-needed basis. They take little or no active management role.

You do not have to take the abdication approach. Instead you can adopt a simple process for deciding what meetings are required:

- *Step 1*

  Identify all the potential management meetings. This can be achieved simply by analysing the work breakdown structure. You should assume that there is a management meeting for each work package and another meeting where there are several tasks being managed collectively.

- *Step 2*

  Decide on the purpose and complexity of each meeting. In many cases the meeting's purpose will be simple. It will involve only the manager and the team member. You should ignore capturing and managing these simple meetings. The meetings should continue but it is not necessary for you to include them in the formal project structure. Instead you should try to identify meetings that are likely to involve six or more people on a regular basis.

- *Step 3*

  You should now classify the identified meetings using the categories given previously: technical meetings, briefing meetings, fun events, management meetings, customer meetings, supplier meetings.

- *Step 4*

  Once all the potential meetings have been identified you should gather together the work package managers. Collectively you and the work package managers should assess the potential meetings. Once you have agreed which meetings are required you should collectively develop a schedule for them. The schedule should cover the frequency of the meetings and their duration. Developing meetings in this collective manner ensures that there is no overlap in scheduling, a common problem in large projects.

- *Step 5*

  Review the agreed schedule for missing meetings. The method of developing the meeting schedule is task focused. However, there are always a number of meetings that add value but are not task based, for example fun events. Where such meetings have been missed they should be worked into the meeting schedule.

The final meeting schedule should now be published and periodically reviewed. It is useful if the meeting schedule is published electronically since this allows it to be updated simply and quickly in response to the changing needs of the project. An obvious place to publish the schedule is alongside the organizational chart on the Web page.

6

Monitoring and controlling the project

Once the project execution phase is established and under way it is important that you are able to monitor and control effectively what is happening. To achieve this you need to consider:

- your management style;
- management of project performance;
- analysis of project performance;
- how you will manage the project interfaces;
- what systems you are going to use.

MANAGEMENT STYLE

Management style varies widely across organizations and within projects. This is particularly true for advanced projects, which frequently involve large numbers of people. The project manager can and does significantly influence the management style used within the project. The style that project managers use with their direct team will be replicated throughout the project. Therefore being conscious of your management style is important since it will enable you to influence the culture of your project. For example, you may choose personally to walk round the team daily to encourage them. Alternatively instead of talking directly to the team you might demand written reports that are accurate and available continuously.

When considering management style you should consider management styles for:

- the project team;
- the external stakeholders;
- the external suppliers.

The project team

There are three basic styles of management that you can adopt: the dictatorial style, the consensus style and the laissez-faire style. All have their merits and problems and all are appropriate in certain circumstances. A good project manager should be able to recognize when a particular style is appropriate. You should be able to adopt that style when it is required.

The dictatorial style is perhaps the simplest style to understand. The style is exactly what its name suggests. The project manager applies a high degree of control to the activities of the staff in the team. He or she specifies on a day-to-day or hour-by-hour basis what the team member should be doing. An example of dictatorial control might be on a building site where a bricklayer is told to put a wall up in a certain place within a certain amount of time. This is very specific and does not require much input from the bricklayer. This style does not involve discussion. Generally speaking, this style is not popular and when applied to teams it can result in things going wrong. When deadlines are tight this style can be used very effectively to achieve successful results.

The most popular style is the consensus style but it is often not understood fully by project managers. They frequently believe that consensus is drawing together people from different areas in the project and asking their opinion. Once they have all the opinions they think that it is their job to decide what to do. This method of working is not a consensus style of management. This style is closer to the dictatorial style where the project manager decides what to do. A consensus style needs to go further than simply seeking opinions. The style needs actively to promote discussion. Ideally the discussion will result in a compromise solution that all involved will be happy to work with. Usually, reaching a compromise can be achieved; however, when it cannot be reached then the project manager may have to move to a dictatorial style. The consensus approach is normally well liked and motivational. The key to a successful consensus approach is to ensure that the discussion and the consensus seeking do not take too long. The purpose of consensus is to assure team members that their opinion is valued and that things can be changed based on their opinion.

Laissez-faire is the third style that project managers can apply. Laissez-faire assumes that every person is motivated to undertake the tasks concerned. It involves low levels of control from a project manager and relies on team members working out what they should be doing. This style assumes that there is a great degree of personal responsibility. People like to be trusted fully and to be given carte blanche to do work in the way that they believe it should be done. Unfortunately this style quickly becomes demotivating. Staff quickly realize that the lack of control contributes to their job being more difficult. This style is not recommended.

What works

When considering which management style to adopt you need to consider how flexible you are willing to be. You will have to apply this flexibility in sympathy with whatever style you choose. Figure 6.1 shows the spectrum of projects that can be undertaken. At one end are simple projects with one or two deliverables. These projects are normally well understood and can be planned

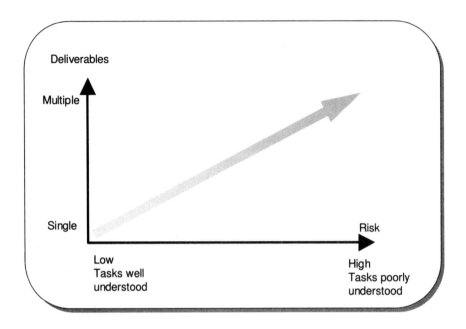

Figure 6.1 Spectrum of projects

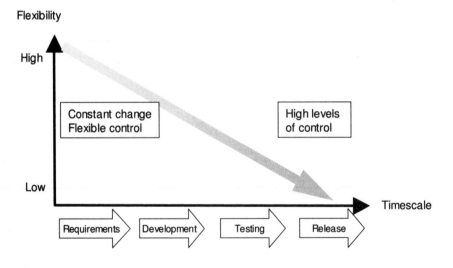

Figure 6.2 Management flexibility needed

with a high degree of accuracy. At the other end of the spectrum are the projects that have multiple deliveries. These projects are frequently poorly understood and planning has to happen on an ongoing basis. These projects are usually the advanced projects.

The management flexibility that needs to be applied to a project depends where in the spectrum, shown in Figure 6.1, the project falls. At the advanced project end of the spectrum, the right-hand side of the diagram, the projects mostly require a flexible style of management. The amount of flexibility that needs to be applied depends on where in the project life cycle the project is. At the early stages a large amount of flexibility needs to be applied since the project is poorly understood and it is still in the requirements analysis phase. At the later stages less flexibility is required since the work tasks that need to be carried out are by now planned. This is shown in Figure 6.2.

The flexibility and the style of management that you should apply therefore are dependent on the position of the project in relation to its life cycle. At the start you must adopt an open-to-anything attitude. You need to encourage others to explore the boundaries of the project. You should try to ensure that all the possible outcomes have been explored. You should be flexible and consensus based in your approach. As the project moves into a planning and definition phase you need to change your style. Now you need to become focused on removing everything that isn't core to the work, which means being more dictatorial in approach. Flexibility will still be required in the definition of the things that are core but those that are not should now be discarded. Moving into the testing and release phases you should become more focused on enforcing the detail of the plan. At this stage you should adopt the attitude and style that are closest to the dictatorial style.

The external stakeholders

Whilst one of the styles discussed is likely to be appropriate for the team involved in the project it is unlikely to be suitable for dealing with some of the more important project stakeholders. Very senior managers are generally only interested in the project for short bursts of time. Their interest is raised when a major milestone is about to happen or when something major has gone wrong. For the stakeholders who fall into this category an exception management style is likely to be most appropriate. Although candidates for this style are normally senior managers, there are many people external to the organization who should also be included. This would include journalists, planning officers, pressure group chairpersons and politicians.

Exception management focuses only on the deliverables and the higher-risk tasks within the project. It centres on these since they are the areas that the target stakeholder group is interested in. The project manager is expected to review and report on anything major that happens in the project. This reporting should not be carried out according to any given life cycle but instead should be driven on the basis of need. For example, if something is going wrong then an exception report should be written.

An exception management style can be very motivating. The style ensures that the key stakeholders and the organization's senior team feel that they are valued. They perceive that they are being singled out for special treatment. This reinforces to them that the project manager has recognized their importance within the context of the project. In return they allow the project manager room to manage the team on what they see as the less important day-to-day matters. This freedom can be very useful for the project manager and it alone often makes using exception management worth while.

The external suppliers

The management style that you should adopt for suppliers should be based on a mixture of the dictatorial style and the consensus style. The mixed style should present the suppliers with a straightforward approach to negotiations, deliverables and other project-related matters. The project manager should emphasize honesty in the relationship with the supplier and should always try to find win–win situations. Most suppliers will respond well to this approach. They understand that project managers have a clear duty to put their own organization first; however, this does not have to mean a difficult relationship. Suppliers, like everyone else, enjoy dealing with project managers who they believe are being fair and honest in their negotiations.

PERFORMANCE MANAGEMENT

Performance and its control is one of the areas on which you should spend a significant amount of time. Sadly, measuring how successful a project is can be difficult, particularly the success of an advanced project. It is difficult to measure success because advanced projects tend to be unique projects. This means that little in the way of previous performance measures exists. Despite the difficulties associated with performance measurement it is nevertheless a goal worth pursuing. The key to measuring and reporting success is to focus on the main foundations of any project:

- timescale;
- resource;
- quality;
- scope.

Once you have understood these and put in place measures to enable their management you need to look at a fifth aspect, performance analysis.

Timescale

Timing is obviously important for any project. However, with an advanced project you need to apply a slightly different perspective. You need to understand what lies behind the timing rather than just the timing itself. Advanced projects by their nature are trying to do something difficult. If they weren't then the project would not be thought of as advanced in nature. This means that although they have a general direction the final deliverable is not always clear. In fact, it is likely to change on an ongoing basis as the project progresses. This effect can be thought of as a funnel (see Figure 6.3).

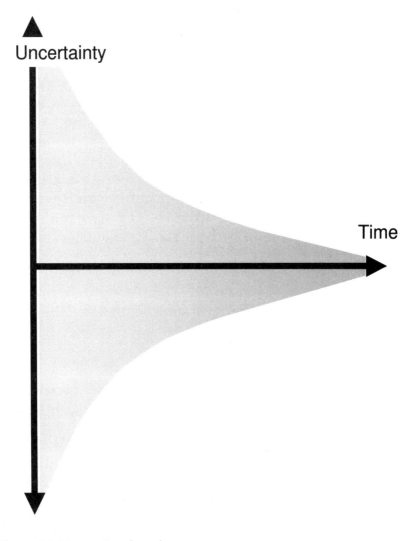

Figure 6.3 Uncertainty funnel

This figure illustrates a lack of certainty at the start of a project, which gradually improves as the project progresses. Put plainly, since you don't know at the start what is to be delivered at the end it is pointless trying to assess it in detail. Instead you should focus on what could potentially be delivered in the timescale. This method is often called a risk-based method. It means that when reporting you should focus not only on progress but also on understanding the end deliverable. A simple way to achieve this is to examine the volume of DLRs against time.

Figure 6.4 illustrates the DLR approach to measuring the likely variation in timescale. The graph shows a sharp increase in the number of DLRs from January to March. This is the initial start-up period of the project. As these DLRs are translated into firm plans in March to April, the rate of increase falls. This happens because there are fewer DLRs being written since the project team is starting to understand the requirements. In March the plan is baselined and work begins. As work progresses there is a steady increase in the number of DLRs. This happens because there are new ideas and there is a requirement to correct existing DLRs.

It is possible to analyse this graph to determine the position of the project. The first measure to consider is the ADLR. This is the number of DLRs that have been created in addition to the baseline. Using this figure in conjunction with the time T1 (time taken for the DLRs to be added), a rate of change figure can be derived:

$$\text{rate of change} = \text{ADLR}/\text{T1}$$

It is this figure that is interesting for measuring the performance in an advanced project. If T1 is held constant then the rate of change can be compared continuously.

Figure 6.5 illustrates a rate of change curve plotted against time. From this graph it becomes obvious that the rate of change increases after June. This is a good indicator to the project manager that action may be needed.

Deciding on the period of T1 depends on the project. If the period is too small then it is not a worthwhile exercise. The graph

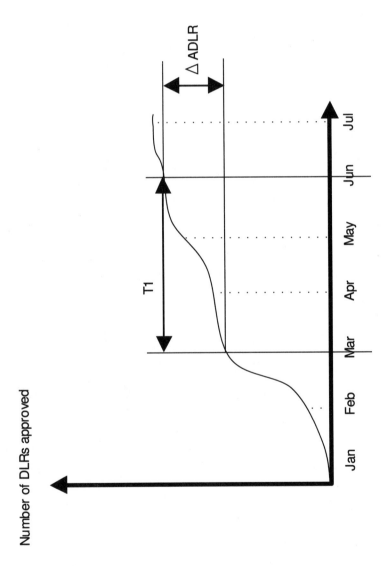

Figure 6.4 DLR volumes

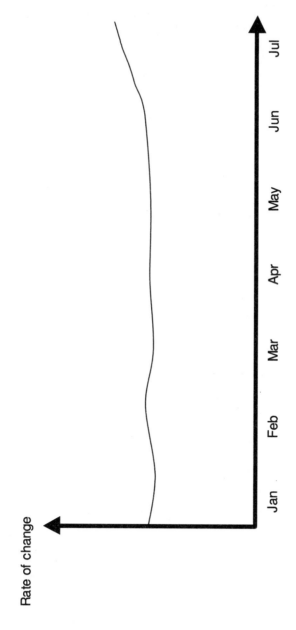

Figure 6.5 Rate of change

will look the same as DLRs against time. However, if it's too large then the rate of change can become meaningless. You should pick a value that gives a reasoned output. You should also not be afraid to change that value if you are not getting the type of result that you want.

Resource

Resource reporting on advanced projects can be complicated. There are a lot of people, and figuring out what they are all doing can be very difficult. If there are 200 people working on a project then you would potentially need to have 200 conversations every day. Obviously some other method or system is needed. Generally, organizations have an in-house system. When this is not the case then you should set up your own monitoring system. Before describing such a system it is worth examining exactly what is required of resource performance measurement.

Resource is employed in two general ways in an advanced project. Firstly, the term is used to cover funds used to buy goods. Secondly, the word is used to mean people who perform activities or services. Both uses need to be measured and need to be included in any performance measurement. Normally interest in these two areas concerns how much of the resource has been used. However, whilst this is an important factor it is not sufficient on its own to measure resource performance.

A simple technique for looking at this is earned value analysis. With this technique the ongoing value is examined as the project progresses.

Figure 6.6 shows two cost lines. The first line is the baseline cost of work performed (BCWP). This is the cost that the project would incur if the project managed to stick exactly to its baseline plan. However, as most experienced project managers know this rarely happens. Therefore a second curve is required. This curve shows the actual cost of work performed (ACWP). In this diagram the cost lines include all costs in the project. However, this could easily be changed to enable the project manager to examine only staff costs or only external consultant costs.

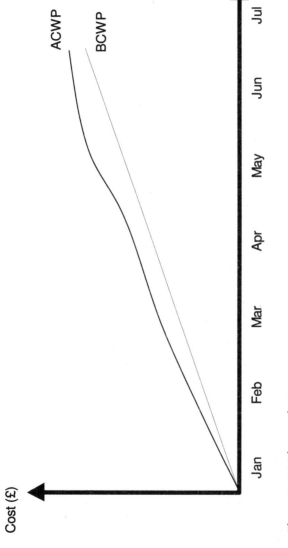

Figure 6.6 Value analysis

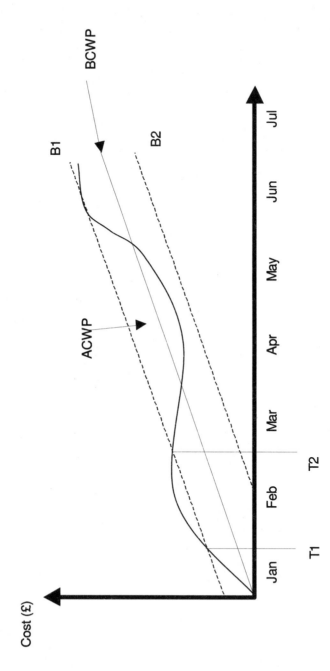

Figure 6.7 Value analysis boundaries

Perhaps the biggest value that can be derived from this picture is the difference between the two lines. This is commonly called the variance, A. The value of the difference at any moment in time is:

$$A = ACWP - BCWP$$

You are able to derive some very interesting data from the value of the variance. If the value is positive then the plan is ahead of schedule. The ACWP line will be above the BCWP line. If it is negative the plan is behind schedule. The ACWP line will be below the BCWP line. However, you need to analyse the chart further before reaching these conclusions. It is perhaps more interesting for you to consider boundaries for the BCWP line and compare these to the ACWP.

Figure 6.7 shows two boundaries, B1 and B2. Examining the figure shows that the ACWP line exceeds the upper boundary B1 at T1. This is the point of alert for you. At T2 the ACWP line comes back within target, presumably as a result of corrective action.

You should also remember that breaking the limit could have occurred not because of problems but because the project was ahead of schedule. However, this might still be a problem in an advanced project because it might affect an organization's cash flow. Cash flow is very important in all organizations. Advanced projects can often form a substantial part of that cash flow. They have large budgets that often run into a value of several million pounds. This can result in difficulties if a project starts to get ahead of its schedule and require funds earlier than expected. For example, it's possible that the borrowing needed to support the advanced project is £5 million. If this money is borrowed too early, extra interest may need to be paid: a lot of interest when you're borrowing £5 million!

To implement earned value analysis, the project manager should simply task each work package manager with maintaining such a graph. The upper and lower boundaries can be set through negotiation. You should not be too harsh in setting the boundaries since they can always be adjusted as the project progresses.

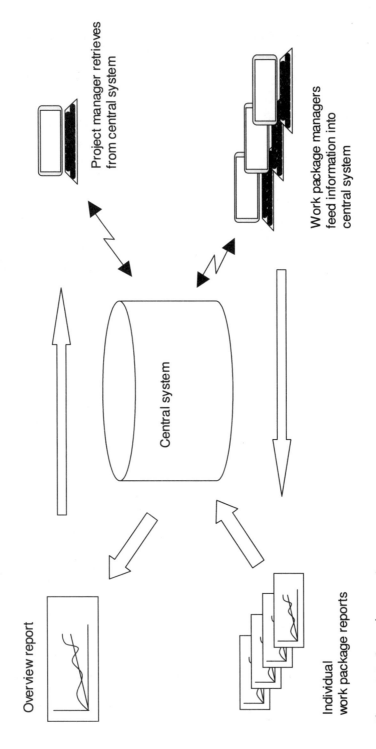

Project manager retrieves
from central system

Work package managers
feed information into
central system

Central system

Overview report

Individual
work package reports

Figure 6.8 Cascade reporting

The graphs that you set up should cover the high level as illustrated. However, in many instances this will not be sufficient detail to allow the type of information that you want. To achieve this, you should set up several graphs to work in a cascade. Cascade graphs can be easily set up using a spreadsheet program. If possible the graphs should be placed on a central server to allow all work package managers access to them (see Figure 6.8). They can then simply update them as needed, removing any requirement for you to collate information. Obviously where this is not possible you or your administrator will need to collate the material.

Quality

Measuring an advanced project's performance in terms of quality can seem a daunting task. Often rather than tackle the issue project managers find a method of avoiding it. It is easier to explain to customers that the organization is quality approved to standard such and such than to explain how quality is measured. Measurement of quality performance does not need to be a difficult task. Put simply, quality should be saying what you're going to do and then showing you have done it.

There are many standards that are commonly used by companies and organizations. Where they exist and you feel they are sufficient they should be used. However, it's worth considering adding some simple quality checkpoints into the system. Quality checkpoints are points in time where a review of the quality is held. There are a few obvious points in time to hold these:

1. macro plan complete;
2. detailed plan complete;
3. at each major milestone;
4. at the conclusion of the project.

At each review you should assess quality and related matters only. You should not get sidetracked into operational matters. For example, when discussing whether the plan is being adhered to, you should not get sidetracked into a discussion on how to bring the project back on to target.

The review should be based on facts. Firstly, the review should consider whether the systems that have been put in place are working properly, for example the boundary conditions set for the cost analysis performance graphs. Secondly, the review should consider whether the deliverables being produced are measurable, for example whether there is a design that is being used as a basis for testing. Lastly, the review should consider whether the staff in the project know and understand the processes and procedures they should be following.

Prior to the meeting you should spend time assessing these issues. If you spend a reasonable amount of time then the meeting is more likely to be productive. At the end of the review a series of actions should be defined. As with all action plans the actions should be Specific, Measurable, Attainable, Realistic and Timely: SMART.

Scope

Measuring performance with regard to scope falls into two categories: current scope and stretch or aspirational scope.

Current scope

Current scope refers to the set of HLRs and DLRs that have resulted from the process used to create the project baseline. Measuring performance for current scope refers to measuring the success of delivering the content of these DLRs and HLRs. This should not be confused with other measures like measuring whether the DLR will be delivered on time. It is important to examine each of the DLRs and HLRs in order to understand fully whether they are being met. It is important to understand this since it is frequently the scope that is reduced to enable the project to continue to hit its time line. This is illustrated in Figure 6.9.

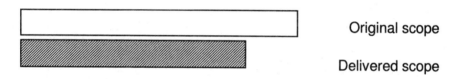

Original scope

Delivered scope

Figure 6.9 Scope reduction

The top bar in the figure represents the ideal scope. The bottom bar indicates the actual scope that is being delivered by the project. This scope is substantially less. Surprisingly this is normal in advanced projects. It is nearly always the case that some part of a DLR will be dropped in favour of on-time delivery. Measurement of this can be a time-consuming activity. It is also not a particularly fruitful activity. Generally customers will only care about final delivery. However, there is a method of examining the project's performance with consideration to scope. Instead of trying to assess the missing scope, project managers should measure the churn in scope.

Scope churn is simply a measure of the change in scope that occurs across the project. It can be easily measured by examining change requests. Scope churn is also sympathetic enough to scope content to make it a useful performance indication. Measuring change requests can give a number of interesting results. In relation to scope the part to examine with the change requests is the number of change requests for any given DLR. However, this on its own is too simple a measure; instead you should be examining the number of change requests raised to reduce functionality. Although this can seem daunting it is actually a reasonably simple task. If it is set up at the start of the project it is also easy to manage. A simple table is all that is required (see Table 6.1).

It is relatively simple for this table to be kept up to date. Perhaps the simplest way of achieving it is to add it to the change request form. It is also advisable to make it a requirement for the body that runs the change requests process to update the table. Scope churn is simply the value plotted out over time. A high churn indicates that the current scope is not stable.

Table 6.1 Change request measurement

Change request title	Reduced functionality	New functionality	Additional functionality
Change request 1	✓	✓	✗
Change request 3	✗	✗	✓
Total	1	1	1

Aspirational scope

Aspirational scope is the addition of new features through the project life cycle. Recording and assessing it is achieved in a similar manner to assessing baseline scope. Space was included for this in the chart of Table 6.1 and appears as the last two columns: additional functionality and new functionality. Additional functionality is based on existing requirements. The objective is to examine the functionality that is added to the initial baseline requirements. New functionality is not based on existing requirements. The objective is to examine how much extra functionality has been added to the project.

Table 6.1 can be enhanced by the addition of a date field. This enables totals to be generated on a monthly basis. This can be tracked as a cumulative graph, as shown in Figure 6.10.

PERFORMANCE ANALYSIS

Many of the measures discussed so far could be classed as general performance measures. To enable you to get the best possible information from these measures you need to examine how you might analyse the results of the measurement. There are several techniques for looking at the various areas:

- comparison;
- ratio analysis;

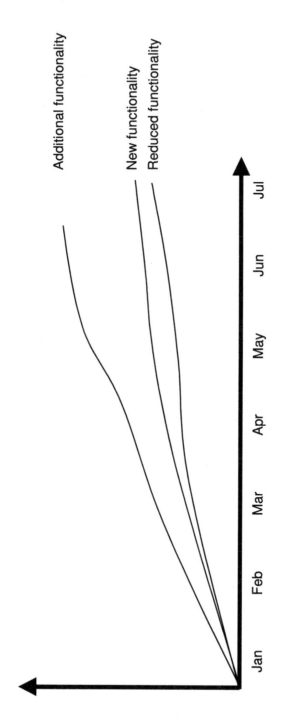

Figure 6.10 Cumulative change requests

- benchmarking analysis;
- historical analysis.

Comparison

Comparison is perhaps the simplest method that can be applied. It simply means comparing the actual result achieved against the baseline plan. This simple technique enables the project manager quickly to identify where problem areas are. To be able to use comparison techniques on an advanced project effectively nearly always requires some level of automation. Automation is required simply to overcome the large volume of tasks that exist.

Perhaps the simplest method of automating comparison is simply to subtract the actual result from the baseline plan. This can be simply achieved by setting up a table in a spreadsheet program; this is illustrated in Table 6.2.

Table 6.2 Subtraction table

Change request title	Actual	Baseline	Difference
Task 1	5	10	5
Task 2	7	3	4
Task n	x	y	x–y

This table is simply created. After it is calculated it is an easy process to sort the results in ascending order. This then gives a list of the biggest variances from the baseline. Subtraction in this manner can be applied wherever there are two data sets. The key is to identify the baseline set and monitor against it. All the areas of the project can be analysed in this manner.

The comparison method can be particularly useful when trying to understand what is going wrong. Analysing data in a localized manner is very often revealing. Analysis like this is especially effective when carried out in an automated manner. Ideally a project manager should narrow down a problem area and then put in place localized monitoring.

Ratio analysis

Comparison of a data set has its limitations. In particular it doesn't allow for the comparison of tasks of dissimilar size.

Table 6.3 Subtraction table tasks of different sizes

Change request title	Actual	Baseline	Difference
Task 1	5	20	15
Task 2	10	100	90
Task 3	5	50	45

Table 6.3 shows three tasks of varying durations. Using the comparison technique it would seem that the task to be monitored is task 2. This may be true. It has the largest number of outstanding days. However, this doesn't allow for a reasoned task comparison. To allow a more reasoned approach, ratios are required. There are several possible ratios:

	Task 1	Task 2	Task 3
Difference:Actual	15:5 = 3	90:10 = 9	45:5 = 9
Difference:Baseline	15:20 = 0.75	90:100 = 0.9	45:50 = 0.9
Actual:Baseline	5:20 = 0.25	10:100 = 0.1	5:50 = 0.1

From the ratio analysis it's clear that task 1 is the most advanced. The analysis also shows that task 2 and task 3 are equally advanced. Tasks 2 and 3 actually are at a similar point, something that comparison alone would have failed to show.

Benchmarking analysis

Benchmarking analysis is simply a term for comparison of an actual result against something similar. As with comparison and ratio analysis, benchmarking analysis can be used in a variety of ways. The most obvious way of using benchmarking in performance analysis is through analogy analysis. This simply means finding the best practice carried out for a similar activity in industry and comparing the project task against it.

Benchmarking sounds a simple enough task but it can prove hard, especially on advanced projects. Advanced projects as their name suggests tend to be new and untried. This in turn means there are few data from which to create a benchmark. To overcome this difficulty the simplest way forward is to set performance guesses. This is done by gathering as much evidence as possible from similar tasks and then guessing what value to use.

Benchmarking however is not only about technical analogy analysis. It is also about the individuals within the project. When examining performance one of the key success factors is staff. Therefore one of the best measures that can be taken is an analogy assessment of staff. This assessment should examine similar activities that were successful and should look at the staff involved. The assessment should cover:

- staff experience;
- staff skill level;
- staff seniority.

Historical analysis

Although benchmarking is a useful technique it doesn't account for the culture of the organization. At the simplest level, the processes used by the organization using the benchmark and the organization creating the benchmark may be very different. This could easily make the benchmark invalid. To overcome this, historical analysis can be used.

Historical analysis examines previous work of a similar nature. It is similar to analogy analysis but normally focuses specifically on data from the sponsoring organization. Focusing on organizational data in this way means that account is taken of the vagaries of the organization. This means the culture, the people and the operating method are all accounted for. Historical data normally have to be tracked down within an organization. A few organizations are however advanced enough to have stored the data ready for future projects.

Historical performance analysis is carried out by using the comparative analysis or the ratio analysis technique. However, unlike in the previous discussions, the only data that would be used are valid organization data. Generally the project manager can have confidence in the results.

There are many ways of examining historical data, too many to examine in this book. However, some basic points apply to them all:

1. Understand what is different about the historical project and the one being undertaken.
2. Understand the changes that have happened in the organization since the historical project, for example whether new processes have been introduced.
3. Ask questions about trends rather than specific details. With historical data this works better since you cannot understand fully the reasons that caused any particular problem.

INTERFACES

Interfaces are the relationships between two or more people within a project. Understanding what is happening at these boundaries is important because it is here that information is passed about within the project. By examining the interfaces you are able to determine what information you are likely to want to know about. Obviously not all of the information passed back to you will be relevant; however, it is relatively simple to set up systems that dispose efficiently of unwanted information.

A more common way of considering interfaces is to examine the stakeholder relationships within the project. This is using the term 'stakeholder' in the very broadest sense. It uses the term to include both project team members and those with any interest in the project and its outcome. Stakeholders fall into two categories, internal stakeholders and external stakeholders. The internal stakeholders are people within the sponsoring organization but normally outside of the project. The external stakeholders are companies, organizations or groups of people outside of the organization. Both groups of stakeholders need to receive and discuss information. However, it is usual for the internal audience to be more directly involved in the project work.

Internal interfaces

Internal interfaces deal with the relationships that happen between members of the project team. Generally this is all of the interfaces that occur inside the sponsoring organization. It is likely that there will be a substantial number of these interfaces. However, each interface will normally fall into one of two groups: either interfaces between groups within the project or interfaces between individuals within the project.

Interfaces between groups within the project are caused by dependencies between different tasks. For example, a test and integration work package will obviously rely on the result of another work package. The other work package will need to deliver to the test and integration work package to allow it to complete successfully. This inter-dependency between work packages is clearly an interface that must be managed effectively. If it is not monitored and action taken when things go wrong, the overall project could be seriously affected. Although the planning will have identified these dependencies, it will not have dealt with the need to manage the dependency interface successfully.

Managing the interface effectively is achieved by examining the resources that are being deployed across the boundary between the work packages. These resources will be people, some kind of material or both people and material. Material might be hardware, software, machinery, etc. The first step in determining what is happening at the interface is to write down all of the information that is likely to pass across the work package boundary. Generally this information is already available from the initial planning. However, it is good practice to review the information with the work package managers of the work packages involved. This review should take place in the context of interfaces rather than a background of simply revisiting deliverables. This will help to ensure a focus on information flow.

Once the information has been identified a chart can be drawn up. This chart should look something like the one shown in Table 6.4.

Creating a chart like this can seem a tedious process that might not add significant value. This is especially true if every piece of information that flows across the interface is captured. However, the creation process does not have to be long or difficult. Good project managers should be able to capture this information as they meet with the various work package managers. The process is simple if a chart similar to the one shown in Table 6.4 is used as a template.

When talking to work package managers you should be careful only to capture information where there may be an issue. You should remember that too much information can be as bad as too little information. With too much information it can be difficult to understand exactly what is going on. Therefore when completing the chart you should triage the information and only include information that needs constant attention.

You should agree a schedule with the various work package managers for the review of the information flows. This schedule not only sets time aside for reviews but it also encourages work package managers to take more interest in other work packages. You need to remember that it may not be obvious to work package

Table 6.4 Information passing across work package boundaries

Originator work package	Destination work package	Frequency of information flow	Importance of information	Description of information	Key dates	Comments
Core application	Integration and test	High	High	Need to assess constantly the ability of the core to pass the mainline assessment	Once every two days	
UI design	Upper application	High initially, low thereafter	High	Design specification is essential	As per work schedule	This is a two-way information stream. The design needs to be sense-checked
Integration and test	Product realization	Low	Medium	Providing information to allow documentation to be produced	As per work schedule	Will become of more significance near end of project

managers that failure to deliver across the interface, on a specific time or to a specific quality, may cause problems. They may view a one- or two-day slip as being acceptable. For example, a team member is working on the software development work package and is scheduled to move on to the test and integration work package. However, the development is running late and the team member cannot be released at the given time. This means the overall timescale for the project slips for every day of unavailability – a simple problem to resolve if captured early enough.

As part of the analysis of the internal interfaces you should look at the relationships between the individuals involved in the work packages. It is often these interpersonal relationships that are the root cause of any interface problems. This can extend beyond simple one-to-one relationships to include teams that do not communicate or try to work together. Analysing the personalities is an area of work that project managers do not often undertake in a formal manner. Instead they have brief discussions to try to figure out who are the 'difficult' people. These 'water-cooler' discussions are not the best way to resolve the problem.

Assessing the personalities

Skilled project managers should be able to apply a systematic approach to identifying personalities and potential clashes within teams. They should be able to categorize the various team members according to personality type. Most project managers will undertake this assessment naturally when they meet team members. This assessment will normally be made at an unconscious level. To enable project managers to apply a systematic approach they need to raise the assessment to a conscious level. This is achieved by adopting a framework within which to rate the various people being assessed. The framework sets out the personality characteristics that you should look for in an individual. The personality types to look for are: idealist, factual, traditional and chaos.

- *Idealist*

  Idealists are people who look for perfection in the work that they do. In a project they are normally the people who are good at the initial requirements setting. They will push others to think continually about what is being produced. These personalities value accuracy and improvement and they make teams focus on producing a quality product.

  Idealists can however cause problems in project teams through their constant desire for perfection. They cause others to despair whether the work they are producing will ever be good enough. Others feel they are being constantly judged and as a result they tend to prefer not to work with idealists.

- *Factual*

  Factual character types base all of their work on facts and the rationale behind the facts. Generally they go into questioning mode very quickly, trying to find out as much information as possible. One of the main benefits of this character type is that it is an action-orientated character type. People with these traits tend to go to work on issues rather than working them through using abstract models.

  Factual people can however be viewed as being aggressive and argumentative. This makes them unpopular, especially if the character trait is strong. Team members often feel threatened by this character type because they are always being asked to justify themselves to this type.

- *Traditional*

  Traditional character types are the peacemakers. They will strive to build consensus and agreement. Often this character type is excellent at chairing meetings or sorting out sensitive issues. One of the best uses for this character type is in dealing with project stakeholders.

  Traditional characters do however fail to push issues forward. Since they do not like confrontation they tend to hold back on pushing others into making a decision. This can make it difficult for the project if they are in charge of a high-risk item of work.

- *Chaos*

  These character types like to be free to do whatever they want. Often these people are charismatic and as a result they enhance a team's motivation. Their desire to be free drives them to be creative and spontaneous, making them very useful at problem solving.

  The obvious negative attribute for this character type is its dislike of any sort of plan. These people believe that it will just happen and that planning is not a worthwhile activity. This makes them extremely difficult to use when a plan must be delivered to a schedule.

Analysing the personalities

It would be very time-consuming on a large project for you to undertake an analysis of the personalities of each team member working on the project. Instead you need to rely on your work package managers for the analysis. You should ask them to look at their teams, using the classification, and then get them to use the characteristics to enable better team working.

In some cases you may find that the character make-up of the team is poor. Perhaps everyone on the team is a chaos character type. When this happens you need to work with the work package managers collectively to move team members between teams to achieve a more balanced team.

External interfaces

External interfaces are interfaces with companies or organizations that are outside of the project team members. The external interfaces fall into a variety of categories: suppliers, stakeholders, partners, customers and other interested organizations. The external interfaces are often as important to the project as the internal interfaces. It is possible that much of the project work will be undertaken by people who are external to the organization. For example, a software company building a new headquarters is unlikely to build the building itself. Instead it would hire architects and builders. When external companies or organizations are used in this way the external interfaces need to be managed effectively.

To ensure that the interfaces are properly understood, the project manager needs to analyse them. This should be done in a similar manner to the analysis of the internal interfaces. This means that the interfaces between the external party and the project need to be identified and listed. Each interface should be examined and the information flow across the boundary determined. This analysis can be undertaken using the internal interfaces chart (see Table 6.4). Wherever practicable this analysis should be undertaken in conjunction with the external company or organization. For example, a supplier may be expecting a delivery from someone within the project on a particular date with a known level of quality.

Once the analysis is complete, both parties should review the information flow description to check that it is correct. They should then determine how they are both going to ensure that the information flow occurs in a timely manner. This might be as simple as a weekly phone call or it may involve a more complex delivery schedule.

The key to managing the interface is to understand the underlying purpose of the interface. The purpose could be simply to pass information across the interface to make the people involved feel informed. For example, building a new airport terminal clearly requires that the people in the surrounding area, project stakeholders, are kept informed. They are not strictly part of the project but they will care deeply about the progression of the work. If the project fails to manage the interface well it could end up with protestors on the airport terminal building site.

Whatever method is chosen, both parties need to remember that the project will change repeatedly. This means that both parties must commit to regularly reviewing the information flow. They need to ensure that the boundary information remains current and useful to both parties.

Reporting

Reporting is an essential part of keeping the interfaces of your project working properly. When the reports are properly conceived they enable you to measure the success or failure of the work being carried out. They also ensure that there is good-quality information available to aid the information flows within the project.

Despite its benefits, reporting is often dreaded by project managers and their teams. They see it as a chore that gets in the way of the 'real' work. Despite how the teams may feel, reporting is an essential part of advanced project management.

Reporting enables those outside of the project to determine what is happening and whether everything is going according to plan. Additionally when it is used effectively it provides a channel for the project manager to pass helpful information to the project team and the stakeholders.

Writing reports

When writing reports authors should ensure they understand who their target audience is. For example, many project managers produce weekly reports for the benefit of their project teams. Then they simply reuse these reports when providing information to stakeholders. They don't account for the different audiences and often the result is problems with stakeholder relationships. You need to take time when dealing with stakeholders. You must understand the audience and the effect the audience can have on the project. You need to understand the type of information the audience wants and the level of detail that is required. For example, it is acceptable to use abbreviations and project 'buzz words' in reports destined for the project team. However, sending the same report to external stakeholders is almost certain to result in difficulties. You would need to include a glossary or similar to explain what everything meant.

There are many types of report required during the lifetime of a project. These range from standard weekly reports to more specialized single-topic reports.

Types of report

Weekly reports

Weekly reports present the progress of the project. They should gather together information about the various project work packages and should provide detail for each part of the project. They should examine how the project is progressing in relation to its overall milestones. The progress report should show the actual plan against the baseline plan and should highlight and explain any differences. It is important that the baseline plan is tracked since it is this that will give an impression of how accurately the project is sticking to its estimated timescales.

You should work with your work package managers to design a reporting system that allows them and you to produce weekly progress reports easily. One of the most effective methods for designing the reporting structure in an advanced project is to design it in sympathy with the work breakdown structure. This ensures that the reporting is based on a project model that the majority of the project readership will not have to learn. Setting up a structure that is sympathetic to the work breakdown structure is straightforward. The project manager should set up a series of reports, creating one report for each low-level work package. This report is then passed to the more senior work package and a summary report created. This is illustrated in Figure 6.11.

WP 2 report = summary of (WP 2.1 + WP 2.2 + WP 2.3 + WP 2.4)
WP 2.1 report = summary of (WP 2.1.1 + WP 2.1.2 + WP 2.1.3)

Reports detailing work package information focus on the output of individual work packages. Each work package is analysed and a summary given setting out the position of the work package. It is important that the work package sets out the information in relation to the original plan. This ensures that the readers understand whether the plan is being successfully executed. The information provided in the report should be concise and clear in its presentation and it should clearly reference the initial work package order.

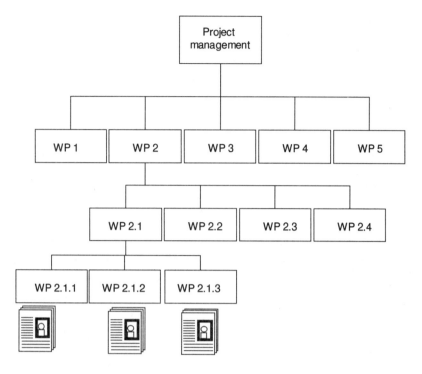

Figure 6.11 WBS outline

Monthly reports

Monthly reports provide a summary of all of the weekly reports that fall due within the month being reported. Unlike the project team members, most stakeholders are working full time on non-project activities. This means that they do not have an enormous amount of time to keep up to date with the project position. As a result they tend to prefer monthly reports to weekly reports. Usually they only want weekly reports when something major is happening or when something has gone wrong. Monthly reports fall into four categories:

● in-depth reports on risks and problems;
● in-depth reports presenting the monthly status;
● general reports;
● overview reports.

● *In-depth reports on risks and problems*

In-depth reports are normally produced in response to a requirement to investigate an area of the project in detail. These reports are designed to enable senior managers or stakeholders to gain a detailed insight into areas that may cause significant problems within a project. The reports concentrate on the high-risk areas within the project and they are usually produced on demand rather than as part of a fixed reporting cycle. Most advanced projects will produce a number of these reports every month covering different topics. The reports can be categorized in two ways: either to assess potential risk or to find out why tasks went wrong.

When the reports are used to assess potential risk they are usually completed in advance of the start of the work being assessed. This normally gives the project manager time to act to mitigate any significant risk to a given task. In-depth reports used in this way are often requested by stakeholders prior to major milestones. When reports are used to assess why tasks went wrong, normally someone outside of the immediate project team undertakes the reporting. Using an independent person helps to ensure impartiality and it is always good to have someone new examine the problem. In-depth reports used in this way are normally requested by the project manager or the project sponsor.

Since this report can cover a variety of topics it is difficult to create any form of standard template. You should ensure that it covers the fundamental building blocks of projects: timescale, resources, quality and scope. Equal space should be given to each area within the report to ensure that a balanced view is presented. The final report should be short and as a result needs to be succinct and clear. You should ensure that authors of reports understand this. They need to appreciate that an in-depth report is not the same as a report that presents every detail of the problem or risk. The purpose of the report is to provide an analysis not to make the reader an expert in the topic area.

- *In-depth reports presenting the monthly status*
  In addition to in-depth reports on risks and problems there are also in-depth reports that present the monthly position of the project. This monthly review gathers together the key information from the weekly reports and presents it in a summary form. This monthly review allows senior managers to review the strategy of the project. Unlike the weekly reports, the monthly report ensures that readers are able to take a 'helicopter' view of the project. This enables them to spot problems that can't be seen from the ground. Additionally it helps stakeholders get a feel for the forward movement on the project, something that is hard to do only reviewing the week-by-week reports.

  This in-depth monthly report and its associated review often becomes one of the most important parts of an advanced project. Frequently it is released prior to the steering group meeting and as a result it guides the focus of the meeting. Issues and difficulties mentioned in the report are almost certain to be discussed. As a result providing accurate information for that monthly review is essential.

- *General reports*
  General reports provide high-level summary information to a variety of people. They supply basic information about progress and deliveries. General reports are most often used for external stakeholders, for the general public or for internal staff information distribution. These reports present information in a very cautious format. They do not offer information that might give the reader a negative impression of the project. Instead these reports are used to present the project to the outside world in a manner that gives those outside the project confidence.

  Unfortunately restrictions sometimes have to be applied to this type of report. These restrictions stop the project releasing information that would explain clearly why things have been undertaken in a particular way. This can cause problems. Barriers to releasing information can occur from a variety of sources. For example, the project may be a secret government project that involves the building of a nuclear power station. Or it may be the destruction of some national monument that will result in a public outcry. Where a secrecy requirement exists it can be very difficult for the project manager to provide public information that is accurate. When this happens you should provide the information that you are allowed to supply. However, you should additionally prepare a strategy for the adverse reactions that happen when the true or full information becomes available.

- *Overview reports*

  Advanced projects regularly introduce a new or advanced concept within an organization. It is therefore important that all the senior management within the organization understand what the project is trying to achieve. When managers are aware of the contents of the project they are able to act as ambassadors for the project within the organization. They are able to explain clearly, accurately and quickly what is happening when they are asked by people who are not working on the project. The final type of monthly report is provided to give support to these managers.

  The overview report's purpose is to educate those senior managers who are not involved in the project. If the report is correctly pitched it can help to ensure that they gain a level of understanding about the work taking place. Overview reports can also be useful to other projects that are either dependent on the project or are working in harmony with the project. Overview reports should provide information that can be 'drilled' through to enable other information to be found. For example, it may discuss a work package and have a reference to a point in the work package weekly report.

If project managers lead reporting effectively they will provide confidence to the people involved in the project. Regular communication that is clear and targeted and is provided on time will enable the project to progress smoothly with the support of its stakeholders. Project managers can drive this communication through the effective use of these four report types.

Risk reports

An integral part of progress reporting is risk reporting. This activity is essential if the project's progress is to be accurately understood. Risks come in all shapes and sizes and this often means that it's difficult to know what risks to report. There is no one simple solution. However, as with many areas of advanced project management there are tools that can help.

Table 6.5 Risk table

Task description	Impact	Urgent
Scope	High	Yes
Timescale	Medium	No
Quality	Low	
Resource		

Table 6.5 shows a simple grid that assesses task risks. As with most areas of advanced project management, this focuses on the fundamentals:

- timescale;
- scope;
- quality;
- resource.

For each fundamental the impact and the urgency of the risk are assessed. You should remember that this tool can only provide an indication of where some problems may be. You should however not rely on this or any other tool. You should remember that perhaps the most important indication of problems is your own intuition. This and other tools should simply be a mechanistic way of sense-checking your intuition.

In an advanced project it is likely that there will be a substantial number of medium and low risks. As a result you should restrict yourself to reporting the risks that are pertinent at any moment in time. This means using your judgement to assess which risks are worth reporting and which risks are not. This can be easily assessed by thinking through how soon the risk is going to affect the project. If it is not going to affect the project in the immediate future then the project manager should probably not report on that risk. Risk reports can become very large if project managers are careless with the information they include. To ensure the reports are meaningful it is important that project managers are judicious with the information they include.

Budget reporting
The major cost in most projects is people. This ensures that it is almost always one of the areas where reporting is required. A simple but effective report is simply to profile the resources against time. This is shown in Figure 6.12.

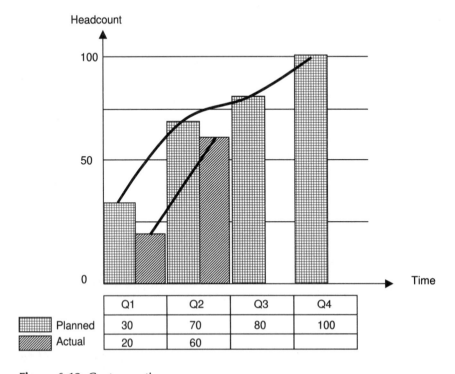

Figure 6.12 Cost reporting

Although this graph presents only a small amount of information it nevertheless is extremely useful to a project manager. Firstly, it enables you to assess the forecast and the actual spend. Secondly, it allows you to anticipate potential problems.

The first use is self-explanatory. You should simply assess on a regular basis whether the spend profile for the project is being achieved or not. If it is not then you need to start to investigate the reasons for failing to hit the profile. Investigation is the second use for the graph. It allows you to determine what is going wrong. This happens when the actual graph is different to the planned graph.

If the actual line is above the planned line then more resource is being spent than was planned. This could have a simple explanation. Perhaps overspend resulted from poor original estimates or work has progressed faster than anticipated and so people have been brought in early. However, the explanation might also be that the project is falling behind schedule and extra resource is being added to attempt to stay on plan.

If the actual is below the planned estimate, again it may be simply poor estimation. However, it may also mean that there are problems. For example, perhaps people are not being used because the work hasn't progressed enough to enable them to start. Whatever the reason the difference in the graph would make you investigate. You must be careful with the investigation since projects rarely hit their estimates. This means that using a precise assessment of the graphs is unwise. Fortunately there is an easy method for overcoming this problem. This is achieved by using tolerance zones similar to the ones shown in Figure 6.13.

Figure 6.13 shows a graph with an upper and a lower tolerance zone. When the project goes outside one of these zones you need to investigate. This simple method can be adjusted depending on the amount of risk the project manager wants to take. A wide zone allows for larger risk than a narrow zone.

Including a tolerance zone has the additional benefit of giving the report's readers reassurance that the risk is actively being managed. It also allows them to assess for themselves whether the

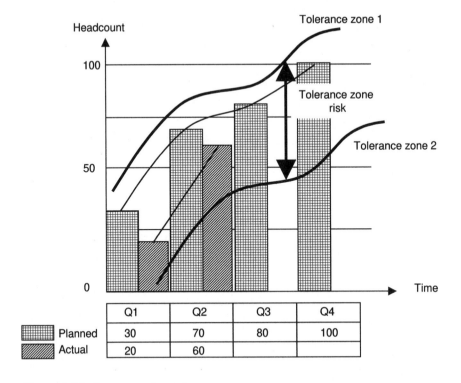

Figure 6.13 Cost reporting tolerance zones

risk being taken is too great or too little. Depending on their views, they can make appropriate representations to you.

Management summary
Management summary reporting covers the top-level activity in the work breakdown structure. It is a summary of all the project reports. Normally the readers of this report are senior managers within the organization who commissioned the project. Unlike the reports discussed so far, this report should not be structured around the work breakdown structure. Instead the report should concentrate on the fundamentals of the project: timescale, scope, resources and quality. For each of these areas the report should explain the current position in relation to the planned position. It should also explain the risks going forward and how they will be mitigated.

Some companies have a standard template for this type of report. Where this isn't available a format similar to that of Figure 6.14 could be used.

Project team information
The final and one of the most important areas of reporting is the reporting of progress to the project team. Ensuring that the project team know what's going on in the project is essential for building clarity, purpose and motivation.

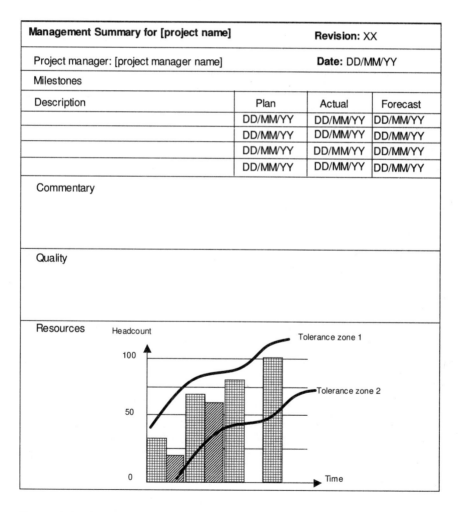

Figure 6.14 Management summary report

Effective communication across a large project team can prove to be difficult. It is not possible for the project manager personally to brief each team member. Instead the project manager needs to rely on the work package managers.

Normally the most effective way of briefing the project team is through cascaded briefings. This should be related to work packages. So the work package manager briefs his or her direct team who in turn brief their team and so on. The project briefing should present the overall picture of the project and then it should concentrate on upcoming activities, their risks and the associated mitigation.

SYSTEMS

Most of the planning and the day-to-day management of projects require extensive use of systems. Frequently project managers misunderstand the word 'systems'. They mistakenly believe that the systems have to be computer based. This is not true. Systems in this sense are the methodologies that enable the support of a particular process or method. They are used to improve control within a project. Some examples of simple systems discussed previously are the work package method and the macro planning process. If a project is to run smoothly, its project manager must ensure that there are appropriate and well-defined systems.

As project managers move through the various parts of a project life cycle they will assess for themselves which systems to employ. It is likely that many of the methods described in this book will be used. The methods will probably be adjusted to fit with the organization sponsoring the project. In many cases the systems will be the organization's own equivalent method and in some cases this will include computerized tools. There are three primary purposes for systems: data collection, information and information assessment.

Data collection

Data collection is the gathering of statistics about events within the project. There are many data sets that a project creates as it progresses. Some obvious data sets are milestones, staff used, staff skill sets, money spent, etc. Many of these data sets have already been defined in the methods described in this book. Each of these data sets, or groups, describes the results of a technique used in the management of the project. The purpose of data collection is to allow analysis of the different data sets that are available. The analysis allows forward planning to become more effective, for example analysing the planned date against the actual date for a particular milestone.

Analysis allows the project manager to assess the four fundamentals of a project, quality, resource, timescale and scope. By examining gathered data you should be able to determine what the status of a particular task is. If the task is slipping then you would be able to determine the size of the slip. However, this is not the main purpose of data collection. The main purpose is to enable the use of trend analysis, which allows you to predict future deliverables based on historic performance. Instead of examining only a single date for the project you should assess many dates. For example, it would be reasonable to assume that if three milestones in a row had been late then a future fourth milestone is also likely to be late. Alternatively if the milestones were delivered consistently on time they may be delivering significantly less than planned scope.

Trend analysis allows future prediction to be undertaken, and indeed programmes such as Excel allow trend lines to be painted on to graphical data sets. The key to undertaking trend analysis successfully is to start data collection in a timely fashion. This means that all estimation and future prediction work is based on the latest data available and therefore the data that most closely reflect the current state of play in the project. Historical data collection can be used to add additional value to data collection about a project. Historic data are data that come from other projects. These data reflect what has happened in the organization. Using historical data helps to enable planning to become more accurate and more effective.

Information

Information flow within a project is essential if quick responses are to be achieved. These quick responses will enable the delivery of the project outputs on time. Systems provide a means of enabling data information flow between different parts of the project. Information is different from data because it provides both qualitative and quantitative analysis. Data can only allow a project manager to achieve a quantitative analysis. Practically, data enable an output that can be graphed and the numbers analysed. A good system will allow information concerning the data (or analysing the data) to be passed in addition to the data themselves. It is essential that the information flow is rapid if action is to be swift and effective. Using systems effectively ensures that information can be available to all members of the project in a simple and rapid form.

Perhaps the most common method of providing information is through the weekly and monthly reports. However, a new medium, the Internet, is now revolutionizing the information flow. The Internet allows problems and issues within a project to be published almost as soon as they happen. The provision of this information in conjunction with the data set can prove invaluable. The information does not have to be in a particular program; instead it simply has to be viewable over a Web browser.

Information assessment

Like data analysis, information analysis relies on the use of trends. Information analysis tries to uncover exceptions and problems that are occurring inside the project. It is especially powerful when things go wrong within the project. Often inexperienced project managers use data analysis and information analysis solely to understand the key metrics behind a project. Frequently this means that they only analyse the scope and timescale metrics. However, information analysis can uncover other trends that can be equally important. Two trends that can be found from gathered information and data that are worth examining are motivational issues and cultural issues.

Motivational issues are often among the most difficult issues for a project manager to uncover. Staff do not like to complain publicly about problems they have; instead their problems are revealed when things go wrong. You can however use trend analysis to overcome this situation. A simple example would be a milestone trend chart. Normally there would be several levels of milestone trend charts. There would be an upper level that shows the overall project, a work package level that shows the individual work package milestone and then sub-projects within each work package. This is depicted in Figure 6.15.

The diagram demonstrates that simply by examining the top-most level it would be impossible to identify any particular motivational problem. However, looking at the lowest-level chart it is clear that the work is consistently late and consistently failing to deliver the quality or the required functionality. Whilst this could simply be down to poor performance and an inexperienced person, it may also be down to a lack of motivation. The chart flags up that there may be some issue that needs to be examined more closely. It allows you to take action if it is required.

Cultural issues can also be identified from analysis. One of the most obvious cultural issues to be examined is the cultural issue between different organizations. When organizations work together often their cultural differences cause problems. Discovering these differences is achieved by examining charts for the work undertaken by the different organizations. For example, if there are two groups, one based in France and one based in London, undertaking work of a similar nature, examining the trend charts for those two groups can be very revealing.

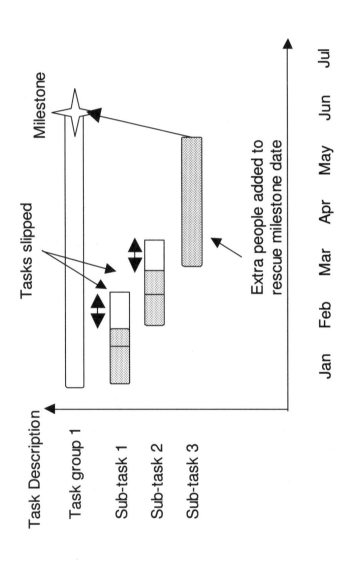

Figure 6.15 High-level schedule hiding problems underneath

Computerizing

In many cases it is sensible to consider computerizing much of the control work of the project. It is very powerful if all of the information can be found in one place. This enables team members to visit that place on a regular basis. If the place is an intranet site then the visitors can be given access not only to data and information but also to forms and templates that support the project methodology.

Before leaving systems and control it is worth while adding a final note of caution. Many projects have failed because they concentrate on the systems and the control rather than on the work that needs to be completed. Project managers frequently spend hours designing systems and improving intranet sites. They are then surprised when they discover that the project is slipping. They are even more surprised when they learn they could have done something about it. Often their reaction is to try to create more systems and more automation. This is the wrong reaction! They need to concentrate on the analysis of the information and the structure and reporting.

7

Successfully shutting down the project

PROJECT CLOSE

Customers of advanced projects are always reluctant to agree to you closing the project. They are nervous about agreeing to the closure because they are concerned that after closure it will become difficult to get problems resolved. Customers correctly assume that the project team will be dispersed and there will no longer be a single point of contact, you, to champion their problem. You need to anticipate this nervousness and deal with it effectively. You can do this by developing plans that demonstrate that customer fears are unjustified. There are four areas that you need to be concerned with: maintenance planning, quality control, post-project review and final documentation. If each of these areas is dealt with effectively then you will be able to reassure your customer.

MAINTENANCE PLANNING

Projects are frequently commissioned with little consideration for the maintenance burden that will occur after the project has completed. Most of the project team will not be involved after the final delivery of the project and they are therefore not greatly interested in the maintenance aspects of the project. You must overcome this disinterest and make sure that maintenance is properly planned. You need to communicate to the project team that maintenance planning is an essential part of the project delivery. Team members should understand that the results of the project may be used for a substantial amount of time. It is essential they realize that, for the sponsoring organization, maintenance needs must be adequately planned.

In many organizations it is a requirement at the start of a project that a maintenance plan is produced. This condition is often driven by principles derived from the organization's quality system. As a result the maintenance plan becomes a prerequisite to passing early milestones. In smaller projects where the scope is well understood, this makes sense. It enables the organization to understand fully the burden that it is creating and to include that burden in any cost analysis. However, this is not always true for advanced projects. In advanced projects, you should treat requests for a maintenance plan at the start of your project with caution. Much of the initial work on an advanced project concerns prototyping and building new, advanced features. These features are not understood until the prototyping phase completes. Therefore it is difficult sensibly to predict the maintenance burden associated with them.

Despite these difficulties it is likely that you will be required to produce a maintenance plan. The sponsoring organization will want to have some indication of the likely maintenance costs. If this happens then you should try to help. However, you should make sure that any plan includes a section outlining any areas where the tasks are poorly understood. As the project progresses, the developed maintenance plan should be reviewed and updated on an ongoing basis.

Many companies have their own templates for maintenance plans. However, there are some common areas that need to be covered in all plans: upkeep and general defect fixing, skills retention and development, identified future work and contractual position.

Upkeep and general defect fixing

This is the area that is normally thought of when project managers are asked to produce a maintenance plan. It involves the work associated with the maintenance and upkeep of whatever is produced at the end of the project. This work ensures that there is a means of fixing minor faults or for making minor adjustments to the outcome of the project. This form of maintenance needs to be accounted for to ensure that the organization is able to keep the outcome of the project up to date. A simple example of this type of maintenance would be painting the exterior of a new building. This is a task that will need to be carried out on a periodic basis after the building project has been completed.

To develop this part of the maintenance plan you need to review the various project deliverables in order to determine whether maintenance post-delivery will be required. If maintenance is required then it will need to be included in the maintenance plan. The simplest method of establishing what maintenance is required is to discuss the deliverables with the team responsible for them. This can be easily achieved by talking to the work package manager of each team. You should ask the work package managers to consider each of their deliverables and to determine whether any post-delivery attention is likely. A simple form can help you gather this information in a consistent format (see Figure 7.1).

Once the information has been gathered you should hold a meeting with the work package manager to review the information provided. At the meeting you should expand on the information in the form. After meeting all of the work package managers you should be in a position to set out a plan for the maintenance and general defect fixing activities.

[Work package title]						Revision: XX			
Work package ID: X.X						Date: DD/MM/YY			
Work package owner: Joe Smith									
Deliverable description									
Likely maintenance needs									
Resources required					Funds required				
Type	Q1	Q2	Q3	Q4	Type	Q1	Q2	Q3	Q4
Skills required									

Figure 7.1 Maintenance of deliverables

Skills retention and development

Unlike upkeep and general defect fixing, skills retention and subsequent development is an area that is often forgotten when writing a maintenance plan. There are three types of skill sets: those the organization already possesses, new skills needed only for the duration of the project and new skills the organization needs both for the project and beyond. When planning maintenance the last skill set is the one that requires the most attention. The first skill set, existing skills, should be dealt with by existing processes within the organization. The second skill set, project-specific skills, will only be needed for the duration of the project and therefore it does not need to be maintained. However, the last skill set, new ongoing skills, is not covered by existing processes and does need to be maintained.

The form shown in Figure 7.1 includes a section asking the work package manager to state what skills are required to support a particular delivery. It is a simple task for you to take this list and transform it into a list like the one shown in Table 7.1.

The number of resources and the different resource types have been identified along the top of the table. These resource types are cross-referenced to the deliverables, which are shown on the left-hand side of the table. This presents, in an easy-to-read format, the required number of resources of a given type. Once the table has been completed you should include the profile within the maintenance plan. If the organization does not have a training or staff development group, you will need to add more detail. This means building training and recruitment plans for the different skills required.

Identified future work

It is extremely difficult for you to complete all of the work that your customer would like you to undertake. Instead you will have to make compromises in order to ensure that the majority of the work is achieved in a reasonable timescale. You will get the customer to agree to these compromises by using the change request process to remove activities that cannot be completed in time. Despite getting this agreement the tasks removed by the compromise process will usually still be required by the sponsoring organization. Effectively their completion is transferred out of the project and returned to the organization's line sections.

Project managers often deliberately ignore the tasks that have been deferred until after the project has completed. They feel that since the tasks are not part of the project they are sensible in ignoring them. They do not want to spend energy tackling tasks that ultimately will not be their responsibility. This is a poor way to proceed. Project customers will be anxious that they have

Table 7.1 Skills review table

| Deliverable | Resource | | | | | |
	System architect	Junior developer	Software developer	Senior developer	Tester	Integration engineer
UI	1					
Core engine		2	3	1	1	
Server engine				1	1	1
Network router	1		1		1	1
Number of people per month	2	2	4	2	3	2

identified tasks that may never get completed. If their concerns are not dealt with effectively then customers will continually seek to get the tasks reintroduced to the project. They will also become reluctant to allow tasks to be removed from the project through change control. It is much better for you to recognize the tasks and take the lead in planning for their completion. This keeps the customer happy and makes managing the relationship with the customer much simpler. An effective way of planning the tasks is to develop a road map that explains the activities that are required during the first year after the project has closed (see Table 7.2).

This simple chart allows customers a reference point to enable them to see what life will be like post-project completion. Its visual impact will enable customers to form a picture in their mind showing what will happen without the project team in place. It shows the work that needs to be completed and indicates an approximate time for its completion. You should develop this chart in conjunction with the customer. This activity should be tackled in a similar manner to the initial work undertaken on macro planning. This means that you will need to develop a work package (see Figure 2.11) for each of the activities. This work package should be signed off and agreed with the customer.

Contractual position

Contracts whose work is undertaken post-project closure are often set up and agreed by you on behalf of the sponsoring organization. These contracts can cover many aspects of the project but most of them are for maintenance activities such as regular building repairs. To help the organization ensure a smooth transition of contracts from project to line unit you should prepare a list of the contracts and their status (see Table 7.3). This will help to ensure that customers feel that they have this aspect of the project under control.

The left-hand side of the form lists all of the contracts that are required and a reference to allow the customer to find greater detail regarding the contract. The right-hand side lists the work

Table 7.2 Simple road map

Q1	Q2	Q3	Q4
Start advertising campaign	Flood channels with software ready for sales	Release upgrade version of software	Fill channels for Christmas sales push
Group ZEE produce plans		Prepare for Christmas sales push	
All work outsourced	Train factory staff Set up call centre	Fix defects reported by customers	

Software released to market

Table 7.3 Contract status

Contract	Reference	Brief work description	Cost

content of the contract and the ongoing cost of the contract. The cost would normally be shown as a complete contract cost but the form can be easily adjusted to account for individual contracts' vagaries.

Not all contracts will be with a group outside of the sponsoring organization. Often contracts are set up between divisions within the same organization. These contracts can be quite legalistic in nature and they are often set up as a service level agreement.

There is no standard format for a service level agreement. They vary in content depending on the company or organization using them. However, service level agreements are all aiming to achieve the same objective. This objective is to state what services one part of the organization is going to provide another part of the organization.

A service level agreement, sometimes known as an SLA, should cover all of the fundamentals of a project. However, unlike in a project, the fundamentals need to be covered from an ongoing perspective. The fundamentals are: resource, which includes the staff costs and any ongoing consumables; scope costs, which contain the minor upgrades that will be required as part of the ongoing costs; quality costs, which relate to the fixing of defects;

and finally timescale costs, which are the outcome of how often each of the costs occurs. Often organizations involve the contract departments in the setting up of service level agreements. This can result in the text becoming long and unnecessarily legalistic. There is no real necessity for this. It is normally much better for a few pages to be drawn up that explain what is required and how often it will be delivered.

QUALITY CONTROL

A part of projects that is often forgotten until the end is certification work. Many projects are required to produce certification at their closure. This ensures that they have achieved a certain standard and are fit for the purpose for which they are intended. Some examples of this might include the certification that proves that a mobile phone is safe for use. Often obtaining such certification takes a number of weeks or in some cases a number of months. It is therefore important to identify the need for this certification early in the project. This ensures that it can be completed in time and as a result the project closure isn't delayed.

At the end of the project there are two stages that are normally undertaken; these are called 'verification' and 'validation'. Often these are completed under one heading called 'acceptance testing'. Verification testing is checking that the final deliverable meets with the specification. Verification is a very important stage in the project. It is the stage where customers agree that everything they asked for has been provided and has been provided to the right specification. For a building this might mean checking that all of the rooms have been completed to the agreed specification.

Verification is often confused with validation. Validation takes verification a stage further and checks whether the project did what was actually desired. The key difference between the two is an understanding that validation is about checking that the customer is happy with the final result. This is an important step because customers, although they may agree that the project has delivered what was asked for, may still be unhappy with the actual result. If this was the case you should take action to try to readjust the project result to meet the customer's expectations. For example, whilst all the rooms may be present and meet the desired specification they may not be suitable for the purpose that the customer has in mind.

The acceptance test is a combination of verification and validation. The acceptance test guides customers through all of the different areas of the project. Initially customers are led through the specification and shown how the specification has been met. Once customers agree that the specification has been met they are then taken through the validation testing. Often the result of validation testing is a list of areas where customers would like changes. The acceptance test concludes with customers signing the test to acknowledge that they have agreed the test is an accurate picture of the project status.

You should not feel that the project is closed simply because the customer signs the acceptance test. You need to demonstrate commitment to your customer. In many cases you will have agreed to undertake activities that have been derived from the results of validation testing. However, viewing the acceptance test as being the test that means the customer is satisfied is a reasonable position to adopt.

POST-PROJECT REVIEW

Post-project review should be very important for all organizations. The review is the organization's opportunity to record historical information for future projects. Additionally it enables organizations to learn from the inevitable mistakes made by the project. Advanced projects by their nature involve the whole company or organization. These projects have a unique opportunity to test the mechanisms within the organization. As a result the review can suggest improvements not only for running projects but also for the way the different parts of the organization operate. This unique opportunity should not be lost by any organization. The organization should embrace it and be frank and detailed about the problems that occurred. For a large project a review could take two or three days and involve a large number of people. If carried out effectively the organization will reap rewards.

However, you must undertake the review with care. You need to ensure that it doesn't become a hunt for people who performed poorly on the project. A good way of holding a post-project review is to use a technique similar to the brainstorming technique described in earlier sections. Groups of people within the project should be invited to a meeting where they are encouraged to brainstorm the problems within the project. Since most advanced projects have several work packages it is good practice to invite one or two members from each work package. These participants should be accompanied by customer representatives.

The different work package members should be mixed together and three or four groups formed. You should take care to ensure that each group represents a cross-section of the people within the project. Each group should be tasked with brainstorming the possible improvements that could have been made to the project. You should brief participants to highlight things that should be done on the next project. You should encourage participants not simply to list everything that went wrong.

Once each group has brainstormed their ideas they should bring those ideas together into a common forum. Often you will find that there is a high degree of commonality between the different groups. You should gather these ideas together and in a second session should work through each of them. Ideally the result of the second session will be a list of positive actions for the organization to take. You should then assign the actions to participants or agree to champion them within the organization.

Post-project reviews should be planned early in the project. When the project starts to reach its conclusion you should seek assistance from the customer to help in setting up a post-project review. Early customer involvement will help to ensure a successful post-project review. Customers will gain a lot of confidence in you because they recognize you are trying to do the best for the organization. It is important that customers have this belief. It helps them to believe that the maintenance planning will have been carried out properly with the interests of the organization in mind. Ideally the customer will not think that you are simply trying to close the project and move on.

DOCUMENTATION

Documentation is frequently an area of project work that is sacrificed to ensure that tasks are completed on time. This is especially true with engineering projects where the team are often not keen on writing documentation. Instead they would rather write thin, brief documents with the sole objective of being able to pass a quality audit. Part of the solution is for project managers to lead from the front from the start of the project. They need to demonstrate to the team that it is important to document accurately the work that has been completed. They need to explain clearly to the people involved that this documentation will be extremely important to those who have to maintain their work after the project has closed.

Getting the team focused on documentation is achieved by focusing their efforts on production early in the project process. This is one of the best ways to ensure it will be delivered in a timely fashion. This means not leaving the documentation until the last two or three months before the close of the project. It requires the team to build documentation production in from the start of the project work. Every work package should include work specific to documentation production. This should include specific deliveries associated with the production of documents. Each of these deliveries should be reviewed thoroughly before the documents are produced. The document review should not begin in earnest as part of the acceptance test. Instead it should be built into the production of the documentation. One method that helps to make sure of success is to involve those people who will have to maintain the outcome of the project. They should act as consultants and reviewers for the team member producing the work. They will be focused on ensuring that the documentation is of the right standard. Care should be taken however in ensuring that the project team remain the authors and owners of the work. Those maintaining the work can often be persuaded by the project team to write the documentation in place of the team member. Whilst this may be acceptable in some cases it is the project team who have the expert knowledge and who should therefore produce the written documentation.

At project closure you should give the customer a complete list of the documentation produced in support of the project. The list should show each of the documents, its title and a brief description. This list can be thought of as being the baseline configuration at the close of the project.

8

Emergency actions

Most of the time, normal project management processes are able to deal with the difficulties that occur in projects. If progress is falling behind, the control system will alert you and you can take corrective action. For example, if the scope is wrong it will be discovered at a functional review and you could take action to revise the scope. However, there are occasions when emergency action is required. This happens when something has gone significantly wrong and has happened in a manner where the normal project process has not alerted you until it is too late to react. In this case you need to put in place a rescue project.

Discovering something has gone badly wrong can be difficult. The reports that you review regularly are summary-level reports. This happens because the volume of work that is required by an advanced project is very large. The large volume of work means that you are unable to understand fully in detail everything that is going on at every moment in time. Instead you have to concentrate on the critical activities and problem areas. As a result, unless the reporting alerts you to a problem then you will assume there are no problems. Unfortunately, reporting sometimes fails. When this happens you need to be prepared. Preparation involves examining four areas in relation to the advanced project being managed:

- working out that things have gone wrong;
- setting up a rescue project;
- working through the available options;
- controlling the rescue project.

This can be considered more simply as: symptoms, implementation, options and control. Preparing these four areas in advance will ensure that when things go wrong you are ready and able to take immediate action.

SYMPTOMS

Searching for symptoms that demonstrate that emergency action is required can be a complex task. There is no one place that you should search. Instead there are various places within the project where problems may be lurking. Regrettably you are unlikely to have time continually to search them all and so you need to look for symptoms of failure. Failure may occur in a task with one resource or a task with multiple resources. The task itself may be small or it may be large and complex. However, in all cases the task should have a plan that sets out what is supposed to happen. It is the plan and changes to it that you should watch. One of the most obvious symptoms of something going wrong is consistent failure. You should be watching for tasks that continually have small deviations from the plan and that are continuously reporting problems.

Finding tasks that deviate from their plan on a consistent basis is relatively easy if the control mechanisms described earlier in this book are in place. These control mechanisms analyse progress against plan and alert the project manager when problems arise. Looking at the ratio of actual plan to baseline plan for the different work packages and their work within the work packages will quickly allow an assessment of where things have gone wrong. Where things continuously go wrong, action needs to be taken.

When you suspect there is a problem you need to be careful in the way that you act. Work package managers when confronted with a consistency problem generally react badly. Rather than deal with the problem they often try to deny the problem. Instead they prefer to try to deal with the problem in private. Their initial reaction is to produce many excuses for the failure and to suggest that contingency and reserve should be used to get the task back on track. You need to cut through these excuses and explain clearly that you have evidence that shows the project is consistently failing. You need to ensure that the work package manager agrees that he or she needs help and that a suitable action plan is required.

There are many reasons why a project might fail. For example, the team may be completely demotivated. They may feel that the work they're doing isn't valued. They may feel unappreciated or simply they may be getting asked to do something that they are not capable of doing. Whatever the reason it is important that you and the work package manager recognize that action needs to be taken. Usually a task that needs rescuing will be on or just about on the critical path of the overall project. It will have reached this point because it will have continuously slipped. For example, it is possible for the installation of a cooker switch to hold up the completion of a new building.

You need to be clear with the team that there are problems. You should resist the temptation to pacify the team by telling them that they shouldn't worry or that these things happen. The team need to understand that they have failed. They have failed to deliver what was needed. Even although this might demotivate the team, you need to be blunt. You should tell the team that performance must improve. The team should be reassured that they will be supported in trying to improve performance. However, they should be left in no doubt that ultimately it is up to them to improve performance and they need to do so quickly. You should undertake this discussion with the team instead of asking the work package manager to talk to the team. This ensures that the relationship between the work package manager and the team is not significantly damaged. It also helps to reinforce to the work package manager that he or she too has failed. You also need to have a blunt conversation with the work package manager. You must explain that the work package manager has failed and now must get things back on track.

IMPLEMENTATION

Whilst briefing the team you are likely to have to answer questions about the reasons for setting up a rescue project. You will need to explain that all other avenues have been tried and have failed. The team are likely to be very vocal in trying to deflect the problems for failure on to others. You in return must be clear and consistent in the message that the team need to sort out their performance. You should not let the team deflect blame on to other people or situations. At the end of the meeting the team should know that there is no more contingency and no more room for failure.

Often at the end of the meeting you will feel drained. You are likely to wonder whether any of what you have said has made any difference. It has. You need to continue to be consistent and not let your personal concerns show to the team. Although the team may not admit it at first, they often already know that there are many things going wrong. Normally they will be very keen on helping to put these things right. Most team members want to add value and they will be keen to help. All they need is some time to get over the initial shock of being told that they are not performing.

Once a failing task has been identified and the team have been briefed that things need to improve, a rescue project should be implemented. This project should be run initially by the project manager and then, once it is delivering to plan, the work package manager.

Perhaps the most important aspect of implementing a rescue project is communication. Communication ensures that everyone knows what has to happen at any moment in time. You should explain to the team that a rescue project is being put in place. Sometimes this briefing can be undertaken at the same time as the briefing where the team are told that their performance needs to improve. However, it is normally advisable to wait for a short time before briefing on the rescue project. This helps to ensure that the team have the message that their performance is poor.

At the initial rescue project briefing you should start by saying that whilst the rescue project is running any problem no matter how small has to be reported immediately. This covers problems with timescale, quality, resource or scope. The team need to be very clear that problems, whatever they are, need to be dealt with immediately. Additionally the team should be briefed to bring up problems continually. If a problem is not being cleared up they should bring it up again and again until it is sorted out. These instructions for the team may seem obvious. However, it is important to vocalize them to the team to ensure that the team feel they have permission to act in this manner.

As time progresses the team need to believe that they have changed your attitude towards them. They need to believe that they have converted you to being a supporter of the team and its abilities. The team need to believe that by working with you their reputation is being restored. You need to convince them that although they have failed in delivering the task there is no lasting stigma attached to the failure. You should explain that you believe in the team. You should tell them that it is for this reason that you are taking a personal interest in sorting the task out. You should point out to the team that they have a privileged position. They are able to cut through all the normal project protocols in order to get things done. There is no reason for failure.

OPTIONS

Now the team have been briefed that a rescue project is being started you must act swiftly to get the project planned and work under way. You must ensure that the team feel a change in pace.

The team need to believe that things have changed and are going to continue to change until the task is completed successfully.

Initially the most important issue for you is to understand the problem. You should examine the task concerned from the four aspects that are the foundation for projects, scope, resource, timescale and quality. Wherever possible you should involve one or two team members in the investigation. This helps to ensure the team will be brought into the final solution.

To examine scope successfully you need to analyse what the initial requirement was. This can be achieved by talking with the project sponsor and the various team members. Since scope is a common cause of failure it is likely that the accounts given by the project sponsor and the implementing team member will be different. Where this is the case you should clarify exactly what is required. You should take care in this process to ensure that they follow the project processes correctly. In this instance this is likely to mean you will need to raise a change request to add or remove functionality. Whilst following the process you should try to find out what went wrong with the process. This should enable you to improve the process to ensure that similar mistakes don't occur again.

Once the analysis of scope has been completed you should examine resource. You should start by understanding what resources were planned for the task. This involves returning to the original estimates and checking how they were developed. Once this research has been completed you should examine whether the planned resource was correctly applied. Applying the correct resource has two aspects: firstly, whether the number of people was sufficient and, secondly, whether they had sufficient experience.

Surprisingly it might not be possible to find out whether the right amount of resource was applied to the task. Although most large organizations have and use time-recording tools extensively, they fail to use them accurately. Staff do not believe in the value of the tool and so often don't put in accurate figures. Therefore when analysing whether the appropriate amount of people have been put on the task it is often more effective to interview the people who were involved.

The second aspect, 'Did the resource have the right experience?', is often a harder question to answer. You must consider all of the team members and their roles. You need to assess whether each team member has the skills and the ability to complete his or her part of the task. A common difficulty, resulting in the formation of rescue projects, is team members being given tasks that are beyond their ability. This does not mean that people are not capable, just that they are not capable at the level required. Where this has occurred you should consider either replacing a person or if possible giving that person more support. Unfortunately it can also be the case that a team member is simply incompetent. Where this happens the team member should be removed.

Analysing problems associated with timescale often ends up being the same as analysing the problems associated with scope and resource. Scope and resource problems tend to result in timescales not being met. This should be evident to you from the analysis of scope and resource. Where there is a clear link you should not spend significant time examining the problem.

One timescale problem that may not have been picked up through the analysis of scope and resource is the task being impossible to achieve in the given time frame. This can occur for a number of reasons that are genuinely outwith the control of the task team. You may find that the team have put together realistic timescales but that circumstances make the task impossible to achieve. For example, the team accurately estimate and submit plans for the development of a software module. The plans state that the work will take one month to complete. The software module relies on a delivery from a company in Sweden. You schedule the work to happen in June and July. The task team suggest a one-month slip on the task. A rescue project is instigated because the task length has doubled. The reason for the slip is Swedish holidays. In Sweden generally most companies take four weeks' holiday in June and July making it impossible in this case for the task team to deliver according to the original schedule. These instances should be relatively simple to find and correct.

Quality is the last factor that you should examine. It is a topic that will have been discussed when analysing the other areas. As a result the analysis for quality should be relatively straight-forward. It is highly likely that you will find that quality has been affected. What you need to assess is why it has been affected. The most likely cause of quality standards slipping is the team cutting corners. Corner cutting will have occurred if the task was signifi-cantly deviating from the baseline and the task team have tried to bring the task back on to the plan. It is often a simple way of making it seem as though the schedule is being adhered to.

Corner cutting is, however, not the only reason for quality slipping. The other reason that is often found is that the task team are unable to achieve the desired level of quality. This may have been picked up during the resource analysis. If not then it should be examined as part of the quality investigation.

COMPLETING THE ANALYSIS

After examining all four areas in detail you should start to develop a plan that will enable the task to deliver to an acceptable time-scale. Generally this consists of either damage limitation or project replanning.

Damage limitation simply means that the task cannot be put back on track. When this happens you must get together the steering group of the project as quickly as possible. You need to explain what has gone wrong, what they are going to do and how they are going to do it to ensure that it doesn't happen again. The plan that you present to the steering group will be a compromise plan. You need to balance the length of time to prepare a detailed plan against the speed of bringing together the steering group. The plan presented needs to give the steering group confidence that the damage to the project is the smallest possible given the circumstances.

When you believe that the task can be replanned you must believe that the project can be put back on track. This is the preferred situation although you need to be sure that the project can be recovered. You also need to seek the opinion of the steering group. Where something has gone seriously wrong you must always inform the steering group. However, unlike in the damage limitation scenario you can probably spend some time pulling together a suitable plan. You can then present that plan at the next steering group. Wherever possible you should try to offer some protection to the task team. This is beneficial, not simply from the perspective of protecting the team, but also because it shows the other team members that they are able to rely on you to protect them even when things go wrong.

One of the questions that the steering group will always ask is whether the task team involved should be replaced. This should have been considered to some extent during the analysis phase but it is worth while analysing the issue in its own right. Often replacing the team is a good idea.

When a new team is brought into a failing project the team members will normally be very enthusiastic. They will feel that the organization has chosen them to come to its rescue. This is very motivating. A new team will also bring a new way of looking at the task. They will not suffer from the preconceptions that the existing team will have. Instead they will start with new ideas and new ways of tackling the task.

The difficulty with bringing in a new team is its effect on others in the project team. Those who were in the original team will still remain in contact with the rest of the project team and they will have a detrimental effect. The original team will tell others that they have been badly treated and that it was all management's fault. However, for you the worst result of this is the original team telling others that it'll happen to them. There is little you can do to stop the original team gossiping but the new team can use their extensive links to explain accurately what is going on.

CONTROL

The final and most important aspect of rescuing a failing task is control of the rescue project. A rescue project should not be treated in the same manner as the other work within the overall project. The team working on the project need to realize in their day-to-day routine that this is a different project to other projects. They need to have tangible methods of working that emphasize speed and control.

The most obvious way of emphasizing the control aspect is to hold daily meetings. These should occur at the same time every day and they should continue for as long as the rescue project is in place. Over the course of the project they will reduce into a short 10- to 15-minute review. The meeting should be based around a series of daily and weekly targets. These targets should be clear and measurable and should be attributed to one person. You should be blunt at these meeting to ensure that the team are very clear about what is required of them. You should ensure that they feel pressured to make sure the targets are met and that the overall task delivers to the new plan.

Despite the time commitment involved in attending and running a daily meeting you should be there personally. Your presence will emphasize to the team that this recovery project is being taken very seriously. Where things go wrong you should step in and help to ensure that they are put right. You should do everything possible to ensure that delivery is maintained.

CLOSING THE RESCUE PROJECT

As a rescue project progresses it should start to deliver consistently and according to its plan. You should be able to sense this happening. There are two tell-tale signs that you should be alert for. The first sign is that the daily meeting is quick and uneventful. The second sign is that everything is delivered on time or early. When this happens it is time to close the rescue project.

Closing the rescue project simply means returning it to the mainstream project. Practically, this involves handing the day-to-day management to the work package manager. This should be done in a controlled manner. The work package manager and you should hold a short meeting. At the meeting you should review the plan and any outstanding risks. You should also review the control methods being applied. All of the review should be recorded in some meeting notes, which should ultimately bear the signatures of you and the work package manager.

Upon formal closure of the project you should take time to gather the project team together and thank them for recovering the task. It is a good idea if you can arrange a small thank-you for those involved. When the closure activities are complete you should ensure that you also inform the steering group of the success.

Index

NB: page numbers in *italic* indicate figures or tables

Goal Directed Project Management
Effective Techniques and Strategies
Erling Andersen, Kristoffer V Grude and Tor Haug

"Well argued and authoritative. . . a very helpful approach to a subject which is central to the business of managing change in modern organizations."
The Work Foundation

"Racy and pragmatic...a worthwhile addition to the literature."
European Management Journal

Goal directed project management (GDPM) is a unique methodology that has been developed and refined by the authors over 20 years. During this period, GDPM has been adopted as a standard approach by organizations all over the world. This fully updated third edition of *Goal Directed Project Management* highlights the close relationship between managing change and the key ideas of GDPM.

The Handbook of Project Management
A Practical Guide to Effective Policies and Procedures
Trevor Young

"A practical, comprehensive guide to be used frequently."
EURONET

This fully updated second edition of *The Handbook of Project Management* is written specifically to help project managers improve their performance using tried and tested techniques. It will be particularly useful if you are: looking to develop project management skills; starting a new project; wishing to acquire new skills; or training others in project management skills.
  The Handbook of Project Management second edition now includes:

- programme management;
- the relationship between programmes and projects;
- new ideas and opportunities for programmes and projects;
- a free CD ROM containing a collection of tools and presentation materials that support the methodology used in the book.

The Practice of Project Management
A Guide to the Business-Focused Approach
Enzo Frigenti and Dennis Comninos

"This comprehensive title will assist anyone who is responsible for converting strategy into reality."
European Foundation for Management Development

Traditional project management has tended to focus primarily on the processes of managing projects to successful completion. To manage projects from their inception through to actual delivery of the business enabling objectives, a different project management approach is needed. Project management needs to become part of the business and, in order to achieve this, organizations need to come to terms with the business of project management. *The Practice of Project Management* addresses the concepts and issues of business project management. It aims to assist organizations in making the shift from a narrow, strong, technical focus on project management to a broader, more business-oriented focus.

Successful Project Management
Apply Tried and Tested Techniques, Develop Effective PM Skills and
Plan, Implement and Evaluate
Trevor L Young

Successful Project Management will enable any manager to significantly increase their projects' chances of success and contains practical and well-tested techniques. This step-by-step guide will help you with:

- project conception and start-up;
- managing project stakeholders;
- managing risks;

- project planning;
- project launch and execution;
- closure and evaluation.

Complete with checklists and specific guidance notes, this essential book covers the entire project management process and will help you get the results you need.

The above titles are available from all good bookshops. To obtain further information, please contact the publisher at the address below:

Kogan Page Limited
120 Pentonville Road
London N1 9JN
United Kingdom
Tel: +44 (0) 20 7278 0433
Fax: +44 (0) 20 7837 6348
www.kogan-page.co.uk

HOW TO USE THE CD ROM

The CD ROM attached to the inside back cover of this book contains a useful Web site that enables you to browse through all the diagrams contained in the book, PowerPoint slides for use in presentations and a text document entitled 'read_me' that gives full operating instructions for using the CD ROM.

Please refer to the 'read_me' document first upon opening the CD ROM. To do this, use windows explorer to navigate the drive with the CD ROM (normally the D:/drive), double click on the CD ROM icon and then double click on the 'read_me' document to open.

Please note: in order to use the CD ROM your computer will need to have an operating system of Windows 98 or higher and a CD ROM drive.